Comprehensible
and Comprehensible and **Compelling**

THE CHEN YET-SEN FAMILY FOUNDATION LIMITED

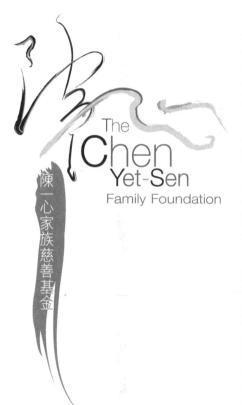

The Chen Yet-Sen Family Foundation Limited is pleased to present this comprehensive exploration of research into language acquisition and literacy development, written by Stephen D. Krashen, Christy Lao, and Sy-Ying Lee.

Krashen, Lao, and Lee have been consultants for the Foundation since 2012, and their research in the promotion of reading, literacy, and language acquisition has hugely influenced our practices. We are very grateful and honored to be working with such dedicated and talented individuals.

This book includes key lessons learned from decades of research, and it is our hope that parents, educators, principals, and academics will take valuable lessons from the evidence presented here, using it to develop their language and reading programs, and ultimately leading to more effective, enjoyable learning for the next generation.

Comprehensible
and Compelling

The Causes and Effects of Free
Voluntary Reading

Stephen D. Krashen,
Sy-Ying Lee, and Christy Lao

 LIBRARIES
UNLIMITED™
An Imprint of ABC-CLIO, LLC
Santa Barbara, California • Denver, Colorado

Library of Congress Cataloging-in-Publication Data

Names: Krashen, Stephen D., author. | Lee, Syying, author. | Lao, Christy, author.
Title: Comprehensible and compelling : the causes and effects of free voluntary reading / Stephen D. Krashen, Syying Lee, and Christy Lao.
Description: Santa Barbara, California : Libraries Unlimited, an imprint of ABC-CLIO, LLC, [2018] | Includes bibliographical references and index.
Identifiers: LCCN 2017028564 (print) | LCCN 2017048241 (ebook) |
   ISBN 9781440857997 (ebook) | ISBN 9781440857980 (hardcover acid-free paper)
Subjects: LCSH: Language and languages—Study and teaching. | Reading. |
   Language and languages—Self-instruction. | Language and languages—
   Study and teaching—Bilingual method. | Language and languages—
   Study and teaching—Orthography and spelling.
Classification: LCC P53.75 (ebook) | LCC P53.75 .K73 2018 (print) |
   DDC 418/.4—dc23
LC record available at https://lccn.loc.gov/2017028564

ISBN: 978-1-4408-5798-0
EISBN: 978-1-4408-5799-7

22 21 20 19 18   1 2 3 4 5

This book is also available as an eBook.

Libraries Unlimited
An Imprint of ABC-CLIO, LLC

ABC-CLIO, LLC
130 Cremona Drive, P.O. Box 1911
Santa Barbara, California 93116-1911
www.abc-clio.com

This book is printed on acid-free paper ∞

Manufactured in the United States of America

Contents

Introduction

The goal of this book is to present the fundamentals of literacy development. The book has seven chapters, but those who don't have the time to read them all need only finish reading the first three paragraphs of this introduction: we acquire both language (first and second) and literacy when we understand what we hear and read, and this happens best when what we hear and what we read is very interesting, or "compelling."

This happens when children (and older folks) hear interesting stories, when they get "lost" in good books, and when they read to become informed about topics about which they are very interested.

This principle, we suggest, underlies successful literacy programs of all kinds. And now the details:

Chapter 1: Compelling Comprehensible Input

We acquire language when we understand what we hear or read, but acquisition happens best when the input is highly interesting, or compelling. When input is compelling, all anxiety disappears, and there is no need for "motivation": language acquisition and literacy development occur without the acquirer realizing it.

Chapter 2: The Three Stages

There are three stages in the development of the highest level of literacy, sometimes called "academic" literacy: (1) hearing stories, (2) self-selected recreational reading, and (3) specialized reading in an area of deep personal interest.

In each stage, the input is compelling. In stages 2 and 3, the reading is narrow: stage 2 readers typically follow favorite authors and genres, and stage 3 readers read because they are seeking knowledge of importance to them.

Chapter 3: What Read-Alouds Do and What They Don't Do

This chapter deals with stage 1 of the three stages on the path to the highest levels of literacy (see Chapter 2). It reviews the research on read-alouds, concluding that read-alouds promote vocabulary and grammar development, and thus promote listening comprehension ability.

Read-alouds also stimulate an interest in books and reading. Studies also show that the language and content of story books can be far richer and more interesting than that found in textbooks.

Some reading experts claim that readers should direct children's attention to the details of the print while reading, in order to help them develop more print awareness and accelerate reading development. Close inspection of the research, however, reveals that interrupting reading produces only small gains in print awareness and may interfere with the pleasure associated with hearing a story.

Chapter 4: Self-Selected Reading

Self-selected reading, stage 2 of the path to the highest levels of literacy (Chapter 2), is often light reading. Extensive evidence shows, however, that self-selected reading results in substantial development of reading ability, writing ability, vocabulary, and grammar. Self-selected reading provides the bridge to "academic" or "specialized" literacy: those who have done self-selected reading find demanding texts far more comprehensible than those who have not.

Chapter 5: Will They Only Read Junk?

Chapter 5 addresses this question: Will children, given the chance to read what they want to read, avoid "good books" and only read "junk"? Our research says this is not so: graduates of "Stone Soup" programs in Hefei, Anhui Province, China, who were encouraged to select their own reading showed somewhat more enthusiasm for reading novels, were equally enthusiastic about reading poetry, and in general were slightly more enthusiastic about reading than comparison students.

Chapter 6: The Complexity Study: Do They Read Only "Easy" Books?

This chapter addresses a related question to that of Chapter 5: Will children, allowed time for free reading, stay with easy books and avoid more challenging reading? Our research, again from Hefei, demonstrates that this does not happen. Judgments of book selections both by teachers and by a group of sixth-grade children revealed that as students mature, they choose more demanding books.

Chapter 7: What Have We Learned from PIRLS?

The PIRLS (Progress in International Reading Literacy) exam is a reading test given to 10-year-olds in over 40 countries (see http://www.iea.nl/). Whenever results from the PIRLS examination are published in newspapers, all but the top one or two countries declare a literacy crisis and demand that schools include more study of the "fundamentals" of reading.

Our goal in this chapter is to determine why some countries (or cities) do better than others. Based on analyses of the PIRLS test from 2006 and 2011, we conclude that the major factors predicting reading scores are poverty (negative) and the availability, and access to, school libraries (positive). This result is consistent with the research reviewed in Chapter 4.

Our results do not support the call for a greater focus on the "fundamentals" of reading. The amount of reading instruction and early literacy development were not predictors of reading achievement at age 10. This result is consistent with current research on the impact of phonics teaching in learning to read in English.

Conclusion

Here we draw together all the ideas from the preceding chapters and point to the implications of our findings. We will do our best.

Compelling Comprehensible Input

1

Compelling input, input that is so interesting that the acquirer "forgets" what language he or she is reading or listening to, is an extremely important factor in language and literacy development: when input is "compelling," only the message exists.

The hypothesis in this chapter is that language acquisition and literacy development are most efficient when input is compelling. If this is true, it radically changes the idea of motivation: motivation to acquire another language or improve in aspects of literacy (e.g., increase one's vocabulary or writing ability) dwindles in importance, and may even become unimportant, when what is heard or read is compelling.

What is important is "the story," or the message contained in the input. When input is compelling, language and literacy development take place whether or not the acquirer is interested in improvement.

☐ *When what we hear or read is extremely interesting, or "compelling," we acquire language whether we want to or not.*

Background: The Comprehension Hypothesis

The most common view of language acquisition and literacy development is that they are the result of " 'skill building." We first consciously learn about language: for reading, this means phonics; for language, this means vocabulary and

☐ *In skill-building, we first consciously learn "skills," then practice them until we can use them automatically.*

1

grammar. We then "practice" the newly learned items by using them in speaking and writing, and refine our consciously learned rules by getting our errors corrected.

The Skill Building Hypothesis is considered an axiom by people who are unaware that there is an alternative view. But there *is* an alternative view, namely, the Comprehension Hypothesis.

The Comprehension Hypothesis states that we acquire language and develop literacy when we understand messages, that is, when we understand what we hear and what we read, when we receive "comprehensible input" (Krashen, 2003).

☐ *The Comprehension Hypothesis says that "skill" development is the result of getting comprehensible input.*

Language acquisition is a subconscious process; while it is happening we are not aware that it is happening, and the competence developed this way is stored in the brain subconsciously. In contrast to the Skill Building Hypothesis, the Comprehension Hypothesis claims that the acquisition of the components of language, the "skills" such as grammar and vocabulary, is the result of language acquisition, the result of obtaining comprehensible input.

The Skill Building Hypothesis is a delayed gratification hypothesis, promising competence only in the distant future, after a great deal of hard work. In contrast, the Comprehension Hypothesis offers immediate gratification: in order for language acquisition to take place, input must be at least interesting so that acquirers will pay it attention. The conjecture is that for optimal acquisition, input should be more than interesting: it should be compelling.

Compelling Comprehensible Input = Flow

As noted earlier, compelling input is so interesting that the acquirer, in a sense, forgets that it is in another language. This process can be regarded as a state of "flow" (Csikszentmihalyi, 1990). In flow, the concerns of everyday life, and even the sense of self, disappear—our sense of time is altered, and nothing but the activity itself seems to matter. Flow occurs during reading when readers are "lost in the book" (Nell, 1988) or in the "Reading Zone" (Atwell, 2007).

Compelling input appears to eliminate the need for motivation, the conscious desire to improve. When we obtain comprehensible input, we acquire, regardless of whether improvement is the goal.

Clear evidence for the Compelling Input Hypothesis includes improvement as an unexpected result. Indicative cases are those who had no conscious intention of improving in another language or increasing their literacy, but simply got very interested in reading, films, or TV programs and made impressive (and sometimes surprising) progress in the language and literacy.

□ *There are many cases of unexpected improvement in language and literacy without instruction or conscious effort. The cause=compelling comprehensible input.*

(1) Accidental Acquisition of English as a Foreign Language in Finland

Jylha-Laide and Karreinen (1993) described the case of Laura, a 10-year-old girl living in Finland who acquired an astonishing amount of English over a four -year period. Laura had no other source of English: English was not spoken at home, and Laura had no English-speaking relatives or friends. Her favorite pastime was watching English-language children's programs, available on cable TV, which she did for several hours a day, focusing on a few favorite programs, all animated cartoons.

Because her favorite programs were only scheduled during the weekend, she videotaped them so she could watch them after school. She not only watched the same cartoon again and again but also had the habit of stopping the video and replaying parts she wanted to see again or did not quite understood. She would watch the same cartoon so many times that she learned a great deal of the dialogue by heart.

Laura began speaking English about a year after starting to watch cartoons. After four years, at age 10, she scored above the ninth-grade level on English as a foreign language (EFL) vocabulary and listening comprehension tests. Jylha-Laide and Karreinen also report that Laura had a near-native accent and had no problems in regular conversation. After an exhaustive description of Laura's grammatical competence, Jylha-Laide and Karreinen concluded that Laura's commend of syntax was near-native.

Jylha-Laide and Karreinen also noted that the language of cartoons was similar in many ways to the language parents and other caretakers use with children: context helped make input comprehensible; speech rate was "relatively low"; syntax was not complicated; and there was a great deal of repetition (p. 121).

(2) Improvement of the Chinese Language through a Compelling Book Series

Daniel's case was described in Lao and Krashen (2008). Daniel was a 12-year-old boy who came from China to the United States at age eight. His proficiency in Chinese was clearly declining, despite his parents' efforts. They sent Daniel to a Chinese heritage language school, but it was clear that Daniel was not interested in Chinese. He was also not an enthusiastic participant in a summer Chinese language program supervised by co-author Lao.

4

When he left the program, Dr. Lao gave Daniel a few books written in Chinese to take home. One was from the A Fan Ti series, in comic book format. Daniel loved it. When Lao learned of this, she loaned Daniel more books from the A Fan Ti series. The books were a big beyond his level, but with the help of the illustrations, Daniel was able to understand some of the text. He was very interested in the stories and begged his mother to read them to him. She read him two to five stories every day. He liked the A Fan Ti stories so much that he would do the dishes while his mother read to him. Both Daniel and his mother were quite happy with this arrangement. Daniel's Chinese was clearly improving, but he wasn't aware of it, nor was he particularly interested in improving his Chinese; he was only interested in the stories.

(3) Third Language Development, Thanks to a Deep Interest in TV Programs

Paul, now a teenager, grew up in a Cantonese-speaking family in California. His parents are both native speakers of Cantonese, but highly proficient in English, and his mother also speaks Mandarin. His grandparents live with the family and speak Cantonese with Paul and his brother. Today, Paul speaks Mandarin quite well, in addition to Cantonese and English. When Mandarin-speaking guests are at his home, he has no trouble conversing on everyday topics, and on occasional visits to China with his family, he is comfortable speaking Mandarin.

Paul's exposure to Mandarin has been nearly entirely through media—TV and CDs—with no classes, no study, and little interaction. His Mandarin input began with a great many cartoons. At age five, Paul and his grandmother watched all episodes of *The Legend of Nezha* (哪吒传奇). At six, he watched *The Winter of Three Hairs* (三毛流浪记), and at eight he watched *Journey to the West* (西遊記) and *The Adventures of Tintin* (丁丁历险记), dubbed in Mandarin. When he was older, he watched movies and TV series such as *Water Margin* (水浒传), *The Romance of The Three Kingdoms* (三國演義), and *Hua Mulan* (花木蘭) with his father on weekends. These Chinese classics, which are not easy to understand even for adult Chinese, were made comprehensible to Paul with the help of his father's explanations, the lively context, and occasional cognates with Cantonese. Every evening Paul watched the TV news in Mandarin with his grandparents.

As was the case with Daniel, Paul resisted instruction in Mandarin. As was the case with Daniel, Paul had no special desire to improve in Mandarin. As was the case with Daniel, Paul was interested in the stories. In both cases, their improvement in Mandarin was a byproduct of exposure to compelling comprehensible input.

(4) A Teenager Who Couldn't Stop Reading

Segal (1977) describes the case of L., a 17-year-old 11th grader living in Israel. L. spoke English at home with her parents, immigrants from South Africa, but had serious problems in English writing, especially in spelling, vocabulary, and writing style. Segal, L's teacher in 10th grade, had tried a variety of approaches:

> Error correction proved a total failure. L. tried correcting her own mistakes, tried process writing, and tried just copying words correctly in her notebooks. Nothing worked. L.'s compositions were poorly expressed and her vocabulary was weak. We conferenced together over format and discussed ideas before writing.

> We made little progress. I gave L. a list of five useful words to spell each week for six weeks and tested her in an unthreatening way during recess. L. performed well on the tests in the beginning, but by the end of six weeks she reverted to misspelling the words she had previously spelled correctly.

In addition, L.'s mother employed a private tutor, but there was little improvement.

Segal also taught L. in 11th grade. At the beginning of the year, she assigned an essay which provoked the following:

> When I came to L.'s composition, I stopped still. Before me was an almost perfect essay. There were no spelling mistakes. The paragraphs were clearly marked. Her ideas were well put and she made good sense. Her vocabulary had improved. I was amazed, but at the same time uneasy.

Segal discovered the reason for L.'s improvement: She had become a reader over the summer. L. told her, "I never read much before, but this summer I went to the library and I started reading, and I just couldn't stop." L.'s performance in 11th grade English was consistently excellent, and her reading habit continued.

(5) An "Avid Reader of English" Whose Reading Habit Got Her in Trouble

Cohen (1997) reports that from the age of 12 she attended an English-language medium school in her native Turkey. The first two years were devoted to intensive English study, and Cohen reports that after only two months, she was able to read in English "as many books in English as I could get hold of. I had a rich, ready-made library of English books at home ... I became a member of the local British Council's library and occasionally purchased English books in bookstores ... By the first year of middle school, I had become an avid reader of English."

Her reading, however, led to an "unpleasant incident" in middle school:

> I had a new English teacher who assigned us two compositions for homework. She returned them to me ungraded, furious. She wanted to know who had helped me write them. They were my personal work. I had not even used the dictionary. She would not believe me. She pointed at a few underlined sentences and some vocabulary and asked me how I knew them; they were well beyond the level of the class. I had not even participated much in class. I was devastated. There and then and many years later I could not explain how I knew them. I just did.

(6) Recovered Dyslexics

Fink (1995/6) studied 12 people who were considered dyslexic when they were young, who all later became "skilled readers." Out of the 12, nine published creative scholarly works and one was a Nobel Laureate. Eleven of the 12 reported that they finally learned to read between the ages of 10 and 12 (p. 273), and one did not learn to read until the 12th grade.

According to Fink, these readers had much in common:

> As children, each had a passionate personal interest, a burning desire to know more about a discipline that required reading. Spurred by this passionate interest, all read voraciously, seeking and reading everything they could get their hands on about a single intriguing topic. (pp. 274–75)

In other words, they found compelling comprehensible input.

How We Acquire Academic Language

We suspect these kinds of cases are far more typical than educators realize. In fact, most of us are examples of similar experiences. Most, if not all, readers of this chapter have developed high levels of academic language competence. Very few of us have "studied" academic language; few of us made deliberate efforts to learn the thousands of words that make up the academic vocabulary; few of us made a deep study of academic writing style; and few of us have consciously studied the grammatical structures used in academic writing. A reasonable hypothesis is that our mastery comes from our reading in specialized areas that we found particularly interesting (Krashen, 2012). We read this material not because we wanted to master academic language, but because we were interested in the content.

☐ *"Academic" language is developed through self-selected reading in our area of interest.*

An Example: The Chinese Summer Program

A rare attempt to supply compelling comprehensible input in Mandarin at the intermediate level resulted in spectacular success, according to what we consider to be truly meaningful measures of achievement.

The program, held in the San Francisco area, lasts for four weeks each summer. The students are middle school age; some are native speakers of English, the children of immigrants to the United States. Others are heritage language speakers of Mandarin or Cantonese and have participated in Mandarin immersion programs in the public schools and weekend Chinese heritage language programs.

The focus of the program is compelling comprehensible input, largely in the form of stories; read-alouds, free time set aside for self-selected reading from a large supply of interesting comic books and graphic novels, watching animations of accompanying comic book series, singing, and engaging in a number of activities of great interest to children of that age (e.g., cooking, making videos), all involving the use of Mandarin.

Old Master Q: The Home-Run Book

Trelease (2001) introduced the concept of the "home-run book" a single reading experience that leads to a permanent reading habit. Three studies with English-speaking children confirm the reality of the home-run book experience (Von Sprecken et al., 2000; Kim and Krashen, 2000; Ujiie and Krashen, 2002). In all three studies, elementary school children were asked one question: "Was there was one book or experience that interested you in reading?" From 50–80 percent of the children said that there was one book that got them interested in reading. In Von Sprecken and colleagues (2000), children were also asked to name the book if they could. Although most simply reported the name of a book, some added commentary, such as:

☐ *Sometimes one very positive reading experience is enough to create an interest in reading.*

> "*Captain Underpants*! That book turned me on, because it was funny and an adventure." "The book that got me interested was *Clue*, because I didn't like to read before." "I liked to read ever since my first book, *Chicka Chicka Boom Boom*." "When I read Garfield books in first grade, I thought I found something better than TV." (Von Sprecken et al., 2000, p. 8.)

For the children in the Mandarin summer program, *Old Master Q* was a home-run book. *Old Master Q* is a series of *manwah* (*manga*, or comic books) with about 150 titles that are simple and easy to read, with many wordless volumes. *Old Master Q* was popular with nearly every child in the program. Those new to the program were introduced to *Old Master Q* each summer by returning students. These books were so popular that a limit was placed on the number of *Old Master Q* books that could be taken home.

Amount of Reading

From *Old Master Q*, children moved on to other reading material. They were encouraged, but not required, to take books home. During the summer of 2011, records were kept of how many books students checked out of the classroom library: the students read an average of nearly 200 books per child, with a range of 100 to 650, during the four weeks the students attended the summer program.

Nearly all the books taken out were graphic novels. This is a staggering amount of interest in reading in a language in which most were not fully proficient.

Only 33 percent of the students (6/18) said they read in Chinese for fun before the program. After the program, 83 percent said they would continue to read in Chinese (15/18).

Parents were amazed at how enthusiastic the students were about reading in Chinese. One mother was concerned because her son dedicated five hours one night to "homework" when the teacher only recommended one hour. The teacher had to explain that the "homework" was pleasure reading and that it was the child's decision to do that much reading.

Several students and parents noticed the difference between the summer class and other, traditional, Chinese classes they had taken. One former student said: "I've been enrolled—or involved for I think three summers, or two and a half years, I guess. And my experience with it is really good because I learned more at this program during my first summer than I probably did in eight years of traditional Chinese schools, Saturday schools." Several graduates of the program, in fact, returned to the class to volunteer and help other students.

Of great importance is that the students developed what we think is an accurate view of how language is acquired, which helps ensure their continuing progress after the program ends. When asked at the end of the summer, "What is the best way to learn Chinese?," students clearly preferred forms of compelling comprehensible input:

Reading	8
Watching movies	7
Listening to songs	4
Singing	2
Writing	1
Using a textbook	1
An encouraging environment	1

The Three Stages

2

It is widely agreed that the goal in all language programs is to develop the ability to use language for more than everyday conversation. This is referred to as "academic language proficiency" and "language for special purposes." In this work, the term "academic language proficiency" is used because it is in common use, but clearly not all advanced levels of language proficiency are "academic."

The approach developed in this book is based on the hypothesis that individuals develop academic language in three stages, in both first- and second-language acquisition, and each stage involves compelling comprehensible input.

□ *The path to advanced language proficiency: the three stages.*

STAGE ONE: Hearing Stories, Including Read-Alouds

Read-alouds and exposure to stories contribute to language proficiency in two distinct ways. First, they provide the linguistic competence that makes reading written text more comprehensible. This includes vocabulary, grammar, and knowledge of how texts are constructed, providing a far richer source of language than textbooks, Second, stories and real-alouds also stimulate an interest in books (for more detail, see Chapter 3).

□ *Hearing stories develops language and gets children interested in reading on their own.*

STAGE TWO: Free Voluntary Reading

Free voluntary reading consists of massive, but not necessarily wide, self-selected voluntary reading. This provides the bridge between conversational language and academic language. The reading achieved in this stage provides the competence and knowledge that will make academic reading more comprehensible.

This idea is consistent with the results of a study by Biber (1988), who analyzed texts in terms of linguistic complexity, and reported that fiction fell about midway between conversation and academic texts (abstracts of technical journal papers).

☐ *Self-selected reading is the bridge to advanced language competence.*

STAGE THREE: Specialized Reading

The free voluntary reading achieved in stage 2 will not bring readers to the highest levels. Rather, it provides the linguistic and knowledge background that helps make academic reading more comprehensible. The remainder of academic competence, we hypothesize, derives from substantial narrow reading of academic texts in an area of great personal interest to the reader.

☐ *At each of the three stages, our goal is not improvement, but improvement nevertheless occurs as a result of hearing stories and reading texts of great interest.*

There is evidence supporting the hypothesis that academic linguistic competence must come largely from reading, with other sources making only modest contributions. It is unlikely that we acquire academic language from classroom interactions or lectures. Biber (2006) reported that classroom discourse is more closely aligned to conversational language than to academic language. Nor, we suggest, does reading assigned texts or studying make significant contributions.

Compelling and Narrow Reading

At each of the three stages, the reading, or input, is compelling, and of deep personal interest. In stages 2 and 3, this generally implies that a process of self-selection has occurred. In stage 1, compelling stories are often chosen in collaboration between the reader and the child. At each stage, the input is narrow, limited to the listeners' or reader's interest. There is no attempt to sample a wide range of texts.

Language improvement is *never* the goal. Rather, at each stage, improvement is a byproduct of the process, as it was in all cases of acquisition via compelling comprehensible input (see case histories in Chapter 1).

A Case History: Author Stephen D. Krashen

My progression as a reader is well known to me and therefore provides a convenient case history.

Stage 1

I began my journey with stories. Growing up in a middle-class home with a large supply of books and a supportive family, I heard stories from, and was read to, by my parents and my older sister. I was also read to in school.

Stage 2

My early self-selected reading consisted almost entirely of comic books. This diet had a far deeper influence on me than anything I read in elementary school. Nearly all the comics were of the superhero type. My friends and I were well aware of each character's strengths and style. We debated the relative superiority of Superman versus Captain Marvel (who would win in a fight?) and decided that Batman deserved extra credit because he was a self-made superhero, neither born with superpowers nor given superpowers by some external agency.

From ages 9 to about 12, I devoured sports novels, especially baseball stories authored by John R. Tunis, who chronicled the struggles of a

15

mythical Brooklyn Dodgers team over a decade. The excitement was the game itself, of course, but also the personalities, the problems each player faced, and their ethical dilemmas. As an adult, I reread the first in the series, *The Kid from Tomkinsville*, and it still offered to me all the excitement and drama it did when I read it as a 10-year-old.

As time went by, my interest extended from baseball stories to science fiction, and my reading remained narrow. I specialized in Isaac Asimov, Ray Bradbury, Robert Heinlein, and my favorite author, Arthur C. Clarke. These authors were very prolific, and I read nearly everything they wrote. As was the case in elementary school, school-assigned reading in high school made very little impact on my reading, whether fiction or nonfiction. My real curriculum consisted of books such as Asimov's *I Robot*, Heinlein's *Have Spacesuit-Will Travel*, and Clarke's *Childhood's End*.

☐ *Each stage can contain several substages. Each substage appears to prepare the reader for slightly more complex reading: comic books helped prepare SK for sports stories and science fiction.*

Stage 3

My history of academic reading is, as was the case with earlier pleasure reading, narrow. The first academic area I read on my own, for my own interest, was the work of Noam Chomsky. I realized early on in graduate school that reading the complete works of Chomsky, in chronological order, was the best way to have a firm grasp of linguistics, that being my field of study at the time. Reading in chronological order, in the order in which the author wrote, made the texts far more comprehensible and turned the reading into a kind of story, a narrative. This approach enabled me to see how grammatical theory had progressed and how Chomsky dealt with problems in the theory. In this way, I absorbed not only much of Chomsky's style but also his method of doing science.

Toward the end of my graduate career, my academic interests changed to brain and language. Once again, I read narrowly and chronologically, working through every study available dealing with left–right brain differences, reading the research on dichotic listening (a method of determining which side of the brain is in use in listening to stimuli), and brain damage and aphasia. My habit was always to begin with earlier studies, working toward the present and focusing on the work of a few researchers. In the area of dichotic listening, I focused on Doreen Kimura of the University of Western Ontario, who, without my realizing it, taught me the essentials of experimental design, the careful and steady progress one can make through carrying out study after study, as well as the academic style of writing experimental reports. When I read textbooks on these topics, they simply confirmed what I had absorbed through my reading of the research. Gaining academic linguistic proficiency was thus not the result of studying "English for academic purposes": it was, rather, the result of self-selected, narrow reading for my own purposes.

An Alternative View

Gardner (2004) has argued that free voluntary reading is largely "light" story reading. Gardner claims that such reading does not contain enough academic vocabulary to make the reading of academic texts comprehensible.

Gardner's evidence comes from an analysis of narrative and expository texts written at the fifth-grade level for native speakers of English. He concluded that the two kinds of texts "are largely dissimilar" (Gardner, 2004, p. 17). His argument is that reading stories will not prepare students for reading academic texts because stories do not contain enough academic vocabulary (subtechnical vocabulary; words such as "academic," "absorb," and "abandon").

Gardner reported that only 7 percent of the academic words that appeared in the expository texts in his sample also appeared in the narrative texts at least 10 times, a number considered to be frequent enough for acquisition to take place.

This is, however, only a problem if one insists that light reading provides readers with everything they need in order to understand every word of the academic texts that they might encounter that year!

This is not the claim of the "self-selected reading as bridge" position, the position that light reading helps make academic reading more comprehensible. The question to ask is whether narrative reading contains enough "acquirable" (more than nine appearances) academic words in it to help make academic texts *in general* more comprehensible, not necessarily those the children might have to read right away.

The answer is yes. There were 338 acquirable academic words in the narrative texts in Gardner's sample. This is an impressive amount.

Gardner's narrative sample contained 1 million words, considered to be what the average middle-class English native-speaking fifth-grader reads in one year. This suggests that a year of self-selected reading will result in the acquisition of about 338 academic words. That is a real contribution, whether or not these words also appeared in the expository texts that the children might read that year.

Gardner (2008) presents a similar argument based on narrow texts, books written by a few authors or on a narrow range of themes. The analysis by Krashen (2011a) shows that the narrow reading texts Gardner analyzed would result in the acquisition of 783 words in one year, about double the figure estimated for academic words from the texts in Gardner (2004), thus confirming the advantage of narrow reading.

☐ *The "light reading" of stage 2, especially if it is "narrow" reading, can result in the acquisition of a substantial amount of academic vocabulary.*

Complexity

Academic language is too complex to be studied and consciously learned. In fact, we do not even have adequate descriptions of academic vocabulary, grammar, and text structure. The existing descriptions demonstrate the complexity of the matter.

Hyland (1996) presents an excellent example of the complexity of academic vocabulary in his thorough discussion of the complexity of the word "quite." Hyland notes that "quite" is both a "booster" (e.g. "the results were quite phenomenal") and a "hedge" or slight attenuation (e.g. "he couldn't quite do it"), but after this simple generalization, things get "fuzzy," as Hyland points out:

☐ *Much of academic language is too complicated to be taught. Specialists in linguistics have not yet provided clear analyses of academic vocabulary, grammar, and text structure, and sometimes disagree among themselves.*

"Quite" varies in meaning according to stress (e.g. "I *quite* like the idea of walking" (but I'd prefer not to), versus, "I quite *like* the idea of walking" (and maybe I will), and whether it comes before or after the article, e.g. "a quite beautiful garden" versus "quite a beautiful garden," the former expressing "greater commitment." He also notes that pedagogical grammars as well as professional linguists differ in their rules for "quite," and notes the inadequacies in their presentations.

Hyland presented data showing that second-year business students at a Hong Kong university had not fully acquired the subtleties of "quite." He acknowledged, however, that the " 'pragmatic complexity' of 'quite' means that it cannot be taught in the usual way: . . . the fact that linguists differ in their preferred accounts of its meanings and implications means that classroom activities based on textbook exercises or intuition-based grammars are unlikely to lead to a clear understanding" (p. 103).

A reasonable prediction is that those second-language acquirers who have better "quite-competence" are those who have read more, especially in self-selected academic texts of personal interest.

It is easy to find other examples. Other scholars have contributed amazingly complex descriptions of grammar, vocabulary, and text structure, recommending that we teach these descriptions to students (see, for example, Swales, 1990; Schleppegrell, Achugar, and Oteiza, 2004).

Acquisition Without Learning

☐ *We doubt that any member of the human race has ever consciously learned more than modest amounts of academic language through the study of English for Academic Purposes or English for Special Purposes.*

We propose that all instances of successful acquisition of academic language are cases of acquisition without learning. We doubt that any member of the human race has ever consciously learned more than modest amounts of academic language through the study of English for Academic Purposes or English for Special Purposes.

We don't deny that people can consciously learn some aspects of academic language. As noted earlier, however, because of the complexity of academic language, it is likely that only a small percentage of academic competence can be consciously learned, and this knowledge is not always easy to access. A useful plan is to determine just what parts of academic language are "learnable" and can be studied with profit.

The assumption has been, however, that all of academic language can be described and then taught. This has been an axiom, not a hypothesis, and has been assumed to be true since the field of English for Academic Purposes began. Both research and everyday experience tell us that there is an easier way.

What Read-Alouds Do and What They Don't Do

3

There is overwhelming evidence that children like to be read to and that many adults enjoy reading to children (research reviewed in Krashen, 2004). There is also overwhelming evidence that hearing stories is very beneficial and that it is the first step toward developing high levels of literacy in both first and second languages.

This section reviews some of this evidence but also makes the point that it is possible to push reading aloud too far, to attempt to make it responsible for developing aspects of literacy that are best done in other ways. If we make unreasonable demands of read-alouds, we run the danger of interfering with their effectiveness.

□ *If we demand that read-alouds do more than they do, we risk ruining their effectiveness.*

Read-Alouds Stimulate an Interest in Reading

When children hear exciting stories, they want to read on their own. The research literature tells us that "storytelling is the bridge" (Wang and Lee, 2007). Children are more likely to select books for independent reading that teachers have read to them (Martinez, Roser, Worthy, Strecker, and Gough, 1997; Brassell, 2003), and children who are read to at home read more on their own (Lomax, 1976; Neuman, 1986).

San Francisco State University researcher Christy Lao (Lao, 2003) asked 22 prospective teachers to retrospect about their reading habits during childhood and adolescence. Twelve teachers described themselves as "reluctant readers" when young and said they grew up in print-poor environments. Only one member of this group was read to as a child. The 10 who described themselves as "enthusiastic early readers" said they grew up in print-rich environments, and all had been read to.

□ *Read-alouds increase interest in independent reading.*

Here is a stunning example of the power of read-alouds to stimulate older reluctant readers, from the third edition of Jim Trelease's *The Read-Aloud Handbook* (1995):

> *Assigned in mid-year to teach a sixth-grade class of remedial students, Mrs. (Ann) Hallahan shocked her new students by reading to them on her first day of class. The book was* Where the Red Fern Grows.
>
> *A hardened, street-wise, proud group (mostly boys), they were insulted when she began reading to them. "How come you're reading to us? You think we're babies or something?" they wanted to know. After explaining that she didn't think anything of the kind, but only wanted to share a favorite story with them, she continued reading* Where the Red Fern Grows.
>
> *Each day she opened the class with the next portion of the story, and each day she was greeted with groans. "Not again today! How come nobody else ever made us listen like that?"*
>
> *Mrs. Hallahan admitted to me later, "I almost lost heart." But she persevered, and after a few weeks (the book contained 212 pages), the tone of the class's morning remarks began to change. "You're going to read to us today, aren't you?" Or "Don't forget the book, Mrs. Hallahan."*
>
> *"I knew we had a winner," she confessed, "when on Friday, just when we were nearing the end of the book, one of the slowest boys in the class went home*

after school, got a library card, took out Where the
Red Fern Grows, *finished it himself, and came to
school on Monday and told everyone how it ended."*

Read-Alouds and Language Development: Vocabulary

An impressive number of studies have demonstrated that read-alouds result in significant vocabulary development, reviewed in Krashen (2004) and Layne (2015). Here are just a few.

Reach Out and Read

Reach Out and Read (henceforth ROR), an inexpensive program based on reading aloud to very small children, has produced remarkable results. ROR is simple: while in waiting rooms for regular check-ups with the pediatrician, hospital staff show parents reading activities they can do with their children, with a focus on reading aloud to the child, and staff members discuss the importance of reading, which the physician does as well. The families receive free books at each doctor visit.

ROR is typically aimed at lower-income groups. Because children in lower-income families typically live in an environment with little access to books, they usually score well below the national average on vocabulary tests. ROR helps close the gap.

☐ *Reach Out and Read is very low-cost, simple, and highly effective.*

In one study of 4-year-olds (Mendelsohn et al., 2001), ROR children had an average of only three pediatrician appointments in which their doctors and the staff discussed books, and they received an average of only four books in total.

Nevertheless, the children made impressive gains in vocabulary, scoring much closer to national norms than did comparison children with similar backgrounds: The comparisons scored about 14% below the norm, a full standard deviation, while ROR children were only 6% below the norm, less than half of a standard deviation: In other words, the ROR children closed about half the gap (see Krashen, 2011b, for a review of additional research).

A Case History

Lee, Lee, and Krashen (2014) reported substantial vocabulary development resulting from a short treatment involving reading aloud and discussing stories with Penny, a child in second grade acquiring English as a foreign language (EFL) in Taiwan. Penny completed eight sessions over one month that included hearing, discussing, and retelling stories. Explanations, sometimes involving the use of Mandarin, were provided when input was not comprehensible.

It was reported that Penny acquired 49 words in 10 hours, averaging 4.9 words per hour, a rate estimated to be about 10 times as fast as learning words through direct instruction in her EFL class.

> □ *Penny, a second-grader, acquired five words an hour in English as a foreign language by just listening to comprehensible stories.*

Grammar, Listening Comprehension, Text Structure, and Knowledge of the World

Chomsky (1972) reported that for early school-age children (age 6), syntactic development was related to how much had been read to the child. Six-year-olds with the highest level of development had heard 17,500 words in read-alouds in one week. Those with the lowest had heard none.

Given the evidence that read-alouds provide grammar and vocabulary, it is no surprise that frequency of hearing stories is a significant predictor of listening comprehension (Senechal and Lefevre,

2002) as well as reading comprehension (Bus, Van Ijzendoorn, and Pellegrini 1995; Blok, 1999).

It is highly likely that hearing stories also contributes to reading ability in other ways: children who have heard more stories, especially read-alouds, will acquire a better sense of how texts, especially stories, are constructed; they will acquire "story grammars." They will also have greater knowledge of the world, thanks to hearing stories. Both of these factors will contribute to better comprehension of texts when the child starts to read.

☐ *Even more benefits of hearing stories: grammar, "text structure," and knowledge.*

Storybooks Compared to School Texts

Hsieh, Wang, and Lee (2011) compared the language found in English storybooks that were read aloud to children in Taiwan with the text-books used in their EFL classes. The storybooks were far richer in vocabulary, syntax, and every-day expressions, and of course the content was much more interesting.

Table 3.1 presents a part of their results: the 65 storybooks used for read-alouds over four years contained about two and a half times as many content words as the textbook series, and far more words of each part of speech.

Table 3.1: Nouns, Verbs, and Adjectives, Appearing in the Stories and Textbooks

Materials	Nouns	Verbs	Adjectives	Total Number of Different Content Words
Storybooks	1073	364	272	1709
H Series	502	128	70	700
J Series	579	145	76	800
L Series	441	102	71	614

Source: Hsieh, Wang, and Lee (2011).

Examination of the sentences used in storybooks and textbooks revealed that the language used in storybooks "is closer to what people would use in their daily descriptions of things, events, and feelings and is thus more interesting" (Lee, Hsieh, and Wang, 2009).

☐ *Storybooks are a far richer source of input than textbooks.*

Table 3.2 presents a comparison of the use of declarative sentences in the textbook series and storybooks. The authors note that in the textbooks, sentences are presented in "an inflexible and mechanical fashion, whereas storybooks present them with richer language and context, thus making the sentences more interesting and comprehensible and thereby providing more input for acquisition, not only of the sentence pattern but of vocabulary and other aspects of grammar" (Lee, Hsieh, and Wang, 2009).

For example, in the textbook by H Series, "The milk is hot" is presented in isolation. The only function of the presentation is to teach the sentence pattern, and there is nothing in the context that makes the sentence either interesting or comprehensible. In contrast, the text in *Winnie at the Seashore*, "It was a very *hot* summer," in addition to presenting the meaning of "hot," also offers the chance for students to make some progress acquiring the past tense and the modifier "very."

Most importantly, it is a story about being at the seashore, which means that there is a helpful context to make the sentence more comprehensible and of course more interesting. This example and similar additional examples are presented in Table 3.2.

Lee and colleagues present similar examples for a wide variety of interrogatives and conclude that "[c]ompared to real storybooks, textbooks present a diminished, weak presentation of

Table 3.2: Comparisons on Statements

Declarative Sentences	Three Textbook Series	65 Storybooks
Word use	The milk is <u>hot</u>. (H Series)	It was a very <u>hot summer</u>. (*Winnie at the Seaside*)
Feelings	I'm <u>hungry</u>. (H Series)	I was real <u>scared</u>. (*Just a Bully*) Miki began to <u>feel uneasy</u>. (*Miki's First Errand*) Elmo doesn't <u>feel sick</u>. (*Elmo*)
Ability or possibility	He <u>can draw.</u> (J Series) <u>Can</u> you dance? Yes, I can./No, I can't. (*DOE*)	I <u>can</u> sail my boat. (*All by Myself*) He <u>can't</u> climb up. It's much too steep. (*Fix It, Duck*)
Days of the week	What day is it? It's Friday. (*J Series*)	Wednesday is bath day for the pigs. (*Giggle, Giggle, Quack*)
Surprise		And you are not going to believe it. (*The True Story of the 3 Little Pigs*)
More complicated pattern		It was time for baseball to start. (*Just a Baseball Game*) Pink is a princess's favorite color. (*The Princess and the Potty*)

Source: Lee, Hsieh, and Wang (2009).

grammar and vocabulary. Story books present a much greater variety of uses and present them in a way that is far more interesting and comprehensible."

What Read-Alouds Do Not Do Well

The term "emergent literacy skills" is generally used to refer to the following aspects of reading competence: "print awareness," defined as familiarity with the alphabet and with the orientation of letters, and performance on tests of "words in print" (knowing words are separated by spaces); "word segmentation" (knowing how many words are in an utterance); "print recognition" (the ability to pick out print when part of illustration); and "print concepts" (e.g., knowing where the title of a book is located).

Table 3.3 attempts to sort out this confusing array of terminology.

Table 3.3: Emergent Literacy Skills

1. Print awareness =
   a. Familiarity with alphabet
   b. Letter orientation
   c. Words in print

2. Word segmentation
3. Print recognition
4. Print concepts

Emergent literacy skills are considered to be a prerequisite to the development of phonemic awareness, phonics, and spelling, which in turn are considered to be prerequisite to learning to read. There is good evidence, however, that phonemic awareness, phonics, and spelling are only prerequisite to the ability to pronounce words presented in isolation, and do not contribute to the ability to understand text (Garan, 2001; Krashen, 2001; Krashen, 2009).

Read-Alouds Do Not Help Children Develop Emergent Literacy Skills

□ *Children naturally pay attention to the story, not the details of the print.*

Senechal and Lefevre (2002) found no relationship between frequency of hearing stories and emergent literacy skills at the beginning of grade 1 (see appendix for discussion of Bus, Van Ijzendoorn, and Pellegrini, 1995). These results make sense; when we listen to stories, the story is the focus, not paying attention to the print, which is not even visible much of the time.

Some researchers are disappointed with this state of affairs and have taken steps that they feel will make read-alouds contribute to the development of emergent literacy skills. In particular, in a series of studies with 4-year-old children, it was claimed that if readers direct children's attention to aspects of print, temporarily interrupting the story while reading aloud, children develop aspects of emergent literacy skills more rapidly (Justice and Ezell, 2000, 2002; Justice, Kaderavek, Fan, Sofka, and Hunt, 2009; Justice, McGinty, Piasta, Kaderavek, and Fan, 2010).

Interruptions consisted of asking children questions and making statements such as: "Where should I read on this page?" "Do you know this letter?" "This word is dangerous." A close review of these studies reveals that interruption does indeed result in more development in some, but not all, aspects of emergent literacy (Krashen, 2013). Most important, however, all the competencies tested appear to be acquired without instruction by children who are exposed to print, and they are acquired quite early. For example, interrupting the story to pay attention to print has a strong effect on a measure of "words in print" (knowing words are separated by a space), but there are few children in first grade who do not understand that words are separated by spaces, and the concept of "word" is firmly established by grade 1 (Knight and Fischer, 1994).

☐ *Forcing children to pay more attention to print may speed development of aspects of emergent literacy that emerge soon enough without this intervention.*

Consistent with this observation is the fact that the comparison groups in these studies also improved, often nearly as much as the experimental, or "interrupted," groups. In many cases, the experimental group scored only a few more items correctly, and the difference in percent gained between the groups was modest.

The Danger of Interruption

Interruption was frequent in the Justice and colleagues studies: verbal interruptions (questions and comments about print) occurred about four times per minute, and nonverbal references (pointing to print) took place nearly 11 times a minute. Combining the two, this means that stories read to the experimental students were interrupted in some way about every 4 seconds. In contrast, the comparison children hardly experienced any verbal comments about print, and nonverbal references to print were made a little more than four times a minute. (Justice and Ezell, 2000).

Justice and Ezell (2000) noted only briefly that excessive focus on print can diminish the pleasure from hearing stories: "[S]ome parents were overzealous in their incorporation of references to print. . . . it is worth mentioning that overuse of these strategies may detract from children's enjoyment of shared storybook reading" (p. 266). This kind of comment does not appear in any of the other studies of interrupting stories, and there was no discussion in any of the studies about how the children reacted to these interruptions, and no discussion, other than the brief section quoted just above, of whether focusing on aspects of print distracted the children from the stories or affected their enjoyment of the stories or their interest in hearing more stories.

□ *Too much focus on print can result in less involvement in the story.*

Children's interest in stories and books is the crucial measure, as story reading stimulates an interest in voluntary reading, and continued voluntary reading ensures continued progress in literacy development. If increasing the amount of focus on print does in fact "detract from children's enjoyment of shared storybook reading," as noted by Justice and Ezell (2000), focusing more on print during read-alouds might disturb the development of literacy.

Conclusions

Read-alouds do a wonderful job of placing children on the path to high levels of literacy. The evidence we have so far indicates that reading aloud to children results in the acquisition of vocabulary and grammar, and may also provide knowledge of text structure and increased knowledge of the world. Children enjoy being read to, and hearing stories increases interest in reading. Also, reading aloud to children is inexpensive. It requires only a good storybook and someone, interested in both the story and the child, who is willing to read the story aloud.

The threat to read-alouds is the desire to make read-alouds do what they are not designed to do, that is, develop low-level literacy "skills." When read-alouds are modified to include instruction in aspects of emergent literacy, there is the danger that the enjoyment of the story will be reduced, as well as the effectiveness of reading aloud. None of this is necessary: children acquire these "skills" without this kind of intervention.

Technical Appendix

Bus, Van Ijzendoorn, and Pellegrini (1995) performed a meta-analysis of studies on the frequency of reading aloud to preschool children. Their results appear to show that frequency of reading aloud results in superior development of emergent literacy, and the effect appears to be quite strong, contrary to the claims made in this chapter.

Table 3.4: The Impact of Reading Aloud

Measure	n	Effect Size
Language	16	0.67
Emergent literacy	16	0.58
Book reading	9	0.55

Language=vocabulary, performance on Illinois Test of Psycho-linguistic Abilities.

Book reading="literacy skills during school age."

Emergent Literacy=reading or writing one's own name, naming letters, phoneme blending.

Bus and colleagues do not indicate which of 16 studies listed in their bibliography were used to calculate the effect size for emergent literacy. Inspection of the studies they list (in their Table 1) produced 13 possible results (in some cases, one study included more than one result, i.e., different tests of emergent literacy were administered). For these 13 studies, the effect size for emergent literacy was 0.57, nearly identical to the results in their table (Table 3.4 above).

In three of the 13 comparisons, the measure of emergent literacy included a reading test. There is good reason to suspect that this component boosted the effect size. In one of the studies, McCormick and Mason (1986), the combined test produced an effect size of 0.87, but in a separate substudy, the emergent literacy subcomponents produced smaller effect sizes (letters=0.29; spelling=0.19, word identification=0.08), while the story component produced an effect size of .94. When the three comparisons that used combined tests were removed, the overall effect size for emergent literacy dropped from 0.57 to 0.44.

One study, Irwin (1960), was a clear outlier, with huge effect. The subjects were very young (less than 2 years old) and the test used was

unusual, measuring the number of phonemes produced in a given amount of time. Eliminating this
study produced an average effect size of 0.32,
down from the original 0.57. Bus and colleagues'
results are now more in line with the hypothesis
that read-alouds do not have a serious impact on
emergent literacy (Table 3.5).

Table 3.5: The Impact of Reading Aloud—Adjusted

Emergent Literacy	*n*	Effect Size
All studies	13	0.57
Without combined tests that include reading	10	0.44
Without outlier	9	0.32

Note: In Mason and Dunning (1986), an unpublished paper, the
results used in the analysis in Table 3.5 included only testing
when the children were only 60 months old.

Self-Selected Reading

4

Self-selected reading is the kind of reading we do because we want to. It is often "light" reading, reading not intentionally designed to inform or make one a better person. The public, as well as some educators, has not held a high opinion of light reading. In fact, light reading has been held in disdain.

□ *Self-selected reading = reading because you want to.*

The Disdain for Light Reading

As Nell (1988) has documented, the disdain for light reading goes back centuries, ever since inexpensive novels were made available to the public. Critics, including Coleridge, condemned light fiction reading as "day-dreaming" (Nell, p. 28) and some even claimed that light reading would cause the brain to "wither away from disuse" (Altick, cited in Nell, p. 29).

In an article entitled "The Evil of Unlimited Freedom in the Use of Juvenile Fiction" Bean (1879), a librarian, claimed that the "craze for books" among schoolchildren leads to "inattention, want of application, distaste for study, and unretentive memory" as well as "utter neglect of home as well as school duties" (Bean, 1879, p. 347). Bean does not provide any evidence supporting these assertions, but her view was shared by others at the time. Graff (1979), in his discussion of "the moral basis for literacy," presents the view of the weekly newspaper, *The Christian Guardian*, in an editorial published on July 31, 1850: "No part of education . . . is of greater importance than the selection of

□ *Often disdained, self-selected pleasure reading is a crucial part of the voyage to higher levels of language.*

proper books . . . No dissipation can be worse than that induced by the perusal of exciting books of fiction . . . a species of a monstrous and erroneous nature" (p. 39).

Many readers have internalized this attitude. Nell (1988) reported that the dedicated adult pleasure readers he studied felt that about half of what they read for pleasure was "trash."

Comic books have been a popular target of disdain: Wertham's book *Seduction of the Innocent* (1954) asserted, without proper evidence, that comic book reading interfered with learning to read and language development. Wertham claimed that "severe reading difficulties and maximum comic book reading go hand in hand, and that far from being a help to reading, comic books are a causal and reinforcing factor in children's reading disorders" (p. 130).

But self-selected reading is just what is needed for the development of high levels of language and literacy. It is a crucial part of the voyage, the bridge from "conversational" language competence to higher levels of reading, to "academic" language competence.

Some Theory

As noted in earlier chapters, the current best hypothesis is that we acquire language in general by understanding messages, by understanding what we hear and what we read (Krashen, 1982). The same goes for literacy: we develop our reading ability as well as our writing ability, an understanding of less common vocabulary, much of our spelling ability, and the ability to use and understand complex grammatical rules by reading (Goodman, in Flurkey and Xu, 2003; Smith, 2004; Krashen, 2004).

Common sense tells us that for reading to make a positive difference, it has to be interesting so that the reader will pay attention to the message. In Chapter 1, we argued that reading has a stronger effect on literacy development when it is not only interesting but also "compelling"; so interesting, in fact, that the reader is not aware of anything but the story or message, and is "lost in the book" (Nell, 1988). When reading is compelling, there is no need to encourage students to read.

☐ *The best way to "encourage reading" is to provide access to compelling reading material.*

Books (and magazines, comics, and blogs) that we read because we are interested in them are, of course, comprehensible and interesting (otherwise, we wouldn't read them), and have a good chance of being compelling.

Supporting Research

Sustained Silent Reading (SSR)

SSR means allowing students to read whatever they want to read in school (within reason) for a short time each day, usually 10–15 minutes. Reading is entirely self-selected, and there is little or no "accountability," for example, no tests on what is read, or book reports to explain or report on what was read. Students taking tests of reading, writing, and vocabulary in language classes (first or second language) that include time for SSR consistently achieve as well as (and usually better than) those students in traditional classes without SSR (Krashen, 2004, 2007).

☐ *The success of sustained silent reading is one of the best-established results in educational research.*

In-school self-selected reading is just as effective for Chinese language material as it is for English. Tse, Xiao, Ko, Lam, Hui, and Ng (2015) reported that fourth-grade children in Taiwan and Hong Kong who reported participating more in independent reading in school scored higher on the PIRLS 2006 reading test, when controlled for students' reading attitude, parents' reading attitude, home education resources, the amount of outside-school informational reading, and the amount of in-class reading aloud by students.

Particularly noteworthy is the explosion of research on SSR in second-language acquisition in recent years, beginning with the work of Warwick Elley and colleagues (Elley and Mangubhai, 1983; Elley, 1991) in Fiji, Niue, and Singapore. SSR has been shown to be effective with subjects at different proficiency and educational levels, and in a wide variety of locations. For reviews of this extensive research, see Krashen (2007); Nakanishi (2014); Cho and Krashen (2015); and for additional sources, see papers at http://c021.wzu.edu.tw/ezcatfiles /c021/img/img/1460/89013_1.pdf, http://c021.wzu .edu.tw/ezcatfiles/c021/img/img/1460/89013_1 .pdf, http://web.ntpu.edu.tw/~lwen/publications .html, http://ks-cho.net/, http://ksmith.bravesites .com/, and www.benikomaso.net/.

The success of SSR is one of the best-established results in educational research.

Case Studies

A number of highly literate people have given self-selected reading the credit for their school success and for helping them develop high levels of literacy. Here are examples:

Geoffrey Canada tells us: "I loved reading, and my mother, who read voraciously too, allowed me to have her novels after she finished them. My strong reading background allowed me to have an easier time of it in most of my classes" (Canada, 1995, p. 89).

According to Richard Wright, fiction helped him become a writer: "I wanted to write and I did not even know the English language. I bought

English grammars and found them dull. I felt I was getting a better sense of the language from novels than from grammars" (Wright, 1966, p. 275).

Lin, Shin, and Krashen (2007) published a case history of a high-school student whose scores on a reading test declined during the academic year but increased during the summers. Formerly an ESL student (her family arrived in the United States when she was in grade 6) Sophia read an average of 50 books each summer, all self-selected fiction, such as the Nancy Drew, the Sweet Valley High, and the Christy Miller series. Self-selected reading during the summer increased her reading test scores, but lack of self-selected reading time at school during the academic year actually decreased them.

In another study, students of English as a foreign language, whose self-selected reading was extensive, improved remarkably on the TOEFL test, a test of "academic language," even though they read different books (Mason, 2006). These students improved on all parts of the TOEFL (listening, grammar, and reading) and made as much improvement per week as those taking an intensive, full-time TOEFL preparation course. Mason (2011, 2013a, 2013b; Krashen and Mason, 2015) has also reported on similar gains on the TOEIC from former EFL students who engaged primarily in self-selected reading for periods ranging from nine weeks to one year.

Correlational Studies

Second-language acquirers who report extensive self-selected reading (referred to as "extracurricular reading" in one study) achieved better results on a variety of measures, including the TOEFL. Self-selected reading consistently emerges as a strong predictor of academic language and typically a much stronger predictor of achievement than do other predictors (Gradman and Hanania, 1991; Stokes, Krashen, and Kartcher, 1998; Constantino, Lee, Cho, and Krashen, 1997; Lee, 2005; Acheson, Wells, and MacDonald, 2008; Krashen and Mason, 2015). Similar results have been reported for reading in Chinese (Mandarin) as a first language: Lee (1996) reported positive but modest correlations between the amount of pleasure reading Taiwanese high school students said they did in Mandarin and their performance on a standardized Mandarin writing test (see also Lee and Krashen, 1996). Also, Shu, Anderson, and Zhang (1995) found that in Beijing, China, third- and fifth-grade students who reported more reading outside of school achieved better results on a vocabulary test of "difficult words."

Hedrick and Cunningham (2002) found that reading also had a positive impact on American children's aural language ability: the amount of reading done by third-graders was a significant predictor of performance on a test of listening comprehension.

A recent report, based on more than 9,500 subjects from the United Kingdom (Sullivan and Brown, 2014), has shown the amount of reading done as an adult is strongly linked to vocabulary development. Sullivan and Brown also reported that those who did more reading as children and at age 16 also had higher vocabulary scores, but the amount of reading done at age 42 predicted vocabulary independent of earlier reading. In other words, continuing to read as an adult counts. Language and literacy development is possible at any age.

Sullivan and Brown also reported that the social class of parents was a strong predictor of vocabulary size when reading behavior was not considered. Once reading predictors were added to the analysis, parental social class variables were no longer significant predictors. This suggests that reading can help overcome at least some of the effects of poverty (for similar results, see also the discussion of PIRLS test results in Chapter 7).

☐ The value of self-selected reading is confirmed by several different kinds of research: It has "convergent validity."

Read and Test Studies

Crucial evidence for the hypothesis that reading provides all the vocabulary we need, comes from "read and test" studies. In these studies, subjects read a passage that contains words unfamiliar to them; subjects are not focused on the new words, and they are then given a surprise test on the words.

Some of the most important read and test studies were administered in the 1980s at the University of Illinois (Nagy, Herman, and Anderson, 1985; Nagy, Anderson, and Herman, 1987). The Illinois researchers used elementary school students as subjects, and passages from elementary school textbooks were used as texts. The researchers' measures of vocabulary knowledge had an important feature: they were sensitive to whether subjects had acquired just part of the meaning of a target word. Nagy and colleagues (1985) concluded from their data that when an unfamiliar word was seen in print, "a small but reliable increase of word knowledge" typically occurred (Nagy and Herman, 1987, p. 26), but this increase was sufficient to account for vocabulary acquisition.

Ku and Anderson (2001) found that for fourth-graders in Taiwan, reading an unfamiliar character in Chinese in context resulted in a modest increase in the ability to recognize the character on a test. This was a similar result to the increase found for reading unfamiliar words in English by native speakers of English. This modest increase, given enough reading, is enough to account for

☐ Those who read more, know more.

43

character knowledge, confirming that reading is the major source of character knowledge.

More Self-Selected Reading Means Knowing More

A number of studies have confirmed that those who do more self-selected reading know more. Seminal studies have shown that free voluntary reading has been associated with extended knowledge of literature and history (Stanovich and Cunningham, 1992), science and social studies (Stanovich and Cunningham, 1993), and even with more "practical knowledge" (Stanovich and Cunningham, 1993). One researcher who summarized a number of studies of the development of creativity concluded that "[o]mnivorous reading in childhood and adolescence correlates positively with ultimate adult success" (Simonton, 1988, p. 11).

Assigned Reading

Readers nearly universally prefer self-selected reading to what is recommended or assigned (Carlsen and Sherrill, 1988): 91 percent of students ages 5 to 17 interviewed by Scholastic agreed that "my favorite books are the ones I have picked out myself" (Scholastic, 2015, and students in sustained silent reading classes (SSR) typically find SSR to be much more enjoyable than traditional instruction (Krashen, 2004). Children do not pay much attention to adult judgment of "quality literature." "Prizewinning" books, as judged by adults, are rarely on lists of books children say they like best or that they borrow from the library (Lamme, 1974; Ujiie and Krashen, 2005, 2006).

The results of a series of studies by Sy-ying Lee showed that self-selected reading produces a stronger effect than assigned reading on language and literacy development for English as a foreign language, even though the teacher-assigned reading was thought to be appropriate and interesting for the students (Lee, 2007).

There are, of course, many cases of readers getting excited about reading because of a book that was recommended; when this happens, the recommendation was just right: the right difficulty level and the right topic (Cho and Krashen, 1994). Even required reading can occasionally help, especially if some choice is allowed. See, for example, Carson (1990), whose mother required him to read three books a week, but the books were of his own choice. Self-selection makes it much more likely that reading will be interesting.

□ *Self-selected reading and "literature" study are natural partners. The Book Whisperer plan is one way to combine them.*

Self-Selected Only?

The case for self-selected reading is *not* the case against the study of literature. The study of literature is at the core of language arts: literature is applied philosophy, dealing with issues of ethics (how should we behave?) and metaphysics (what are we doing here?) that are often made clearer when presented in the context of a story. Literature study thus means intense problem solving, which results in cognitive development as well as literacy development. An added dividend is that exposure to books in literature classes should result in more self-selected reading.

As noted above, recommended and assigned reading can work when the conditions are right.

Literature: Some Suggestions

There have been some magnificent suggestions for basing the study of literature on self-selected material, and descriptions of these programs are very exciting.

In *The Book Whisperer*, Miller (2009) presents her plan, designed for students of English language arts in the United States at the middle school level, but applicable to many language education programs. The focus of the class is on literature, but students choose which items they want to read. If, for example, the topic is the historical novel, students can choose the historical novel (or novels) they read. This guarantees at least a reasonable level of interest and results in stimulating classroom discussions, as students will have had somewhat different reading experiences. Miller reports that her middle school students in this kind of program are required to read about 40 books during the school year. Those who read the 40 books always read more. Atwell (2007) describes a similar plan and reports that it results in students entering "the reading zone," the complete absorption that occurs when reading is compelling.

Will They Only Read Junk?

In the previous chapter, we presented evidence that when allowed to select their own reading, readers make excellent progress in literacy both in first and second languages. But there are concerns with self-selected reading. Some educators and parents fear that if we allow children to read what they like, they will avoid literature of high quality and will have no interest in reading classics and nonfiction. There is no evidence that this kind of "light reading" is bad for language and literacy development: in fact, as noted above, study after study shows that self-selected reading leads to very good language and literacy development. Nevertheless, it is of interest to see whether books selected by those who have read a great deal of self-selected material are of low perceived quality. The only previous study we are aware of that deals with this question is Schoonover (1938), who reported that those who participate in self-selected reading programs eventually choose what experts had decided were "good books."

□ *Although "light reading" is good for you, we want to know if young readers eventually read more "serious" literature.*

To see if this was the case, we examined the reading preferences of seventh-graders who were graduates of an elementary school in Hefei, China, and compared them to seventh-graders who had a traditional elementary school experience.

Experimental students had all attended schools that were part of the Stone Soup Happy Reading Alliance (SSHRA), funded by the Hong Kong–based Chen Yet-Sen Family Foundation Limited. As described in detail by Gordon (2014),

□ *We compared Stone Soup graduates, who had done lots of self-selected reading, and students from a more traditional background.*

SSHRA provides 30 minutes a day for self-selected reading, regular read-aloud sessions, including sessions in which the principal reads aloud to the children, and a wide variety of literacy activities. Most important, books are readily available, not just in classrooms and the library but also in hallways.

The study intended to investigate whether Stone Soup graduates would have less interest in reading classics and more interest in reading popular literature and comics, as compared to students in traditional comparison schools. The study also sought to determine whether those experiencing the Stone Soup program would show more positive attitudes toward reading in general after finishing the program.

Students in seven classes (sample sizes presented in Table 5.1) completed a questionnaire probing their reading preferences.

Table 5.1: Sample Size

Class	Sample size	Comparison
1	14	18
2	16	17
3	22	20
4	17	19
5	8	16
6	13	23
7	10	10

The questionnaire was presented in Mandarin. An English translation with key words in Mandarin is presented below:

If you could read anything you wanted to read, what would it be?

1. Picture books (图画书) (1) yes, for sure; (2) somewhat interested; (3) not interested

2. Comics (漫画书) (1) yes, for sure; (2) somewhat interested; (3) not interested

3. Novels (小说) (1) yes, for sure; (2) somewhat interested; (3) not interested

4. Poetry (诗选集) (1) yes, for sure; (2) somewhat interested; (3) not interested

5. Classics (经典文学) (1) yes, for sure; (2) somewhat interested; (3) not interested

6. Textbooks (教科书) (1) yes, for sure; (2) somewhat interested; (3) not interested

7. Life style, recreational (休闲娱乐生活相关杂志) (1) yes, for sure; (2) somewhat interested; (3) not interested

8. Nonfiction and informational books and magazines (资讯科学相关之书 籍/杂志) (1) yes, for sure; (2) somewhat interested; (3) not interested

A response of "yes, for sure" was scored as 1; "somewhat interested" as 2; and "not interested" was scored as "3" points. Thus, a lower score indicates more interest.

Results

Table 5.2 tells us that the Stone Soup group was more interested in all genres except poetry, where there was no difference between the groups, and textbooks.

As presented in Table 5.2, for both groups, the most popular reading material was novels, informational/magazine reading, and classics, with picture books and comics the least popular.

The rankings of Stone Soup graduates and comparisons were highly correlated (*r*=0.92): in

Table 5.2: Means for Each Genre (Classes Combined)

Genre	Stone Soup	Comparisons	t-Score	p-Level	Effect Size
Classics	1.58 (0.25)	1.76 (0.36)	1.31	0.24	0.59
Textbooks	1.98 (0.32)	1.84 (0.25)	0.79	0.46	−0.32
Poetry	1.98 (0.2)	1.98 (0.15)	0	1.0	0
Novels	1.57 (0.36)	1.73 (0.31)	1.87	0.111	0.48
Informational	1.57 (0.18)	1.67 (0.19)	1.06	0.31	0.54
Life style	1.89 (0.33)	2.04 (0.34)	1.27	0.25	0.45
Comics	2.08 (0.16)	2.29 (0.16)	3.26	0.017	1.31
Picture books	2.34 (0.16)	2.5 (0.12)	1.86	0.111	0.61

Note: Table 5.2 contains a column with the label "Effect Size." Effect size is a valuable statistic that tells us, simply, the size of the effect. A positive effect size means that the Stone Soup group was more interested in reading a particular genre than the comparison group was. An effect size of 0.2 is considered small; 0.5 is considered medium; and 0.8 or larger is a large effect size.

□ *In general. Stone Soup graduates were more enthusiastic about reading.*

□ *Stone Soup graduates were more enthusiastic than comparisons about reading in nearly all categories, from the heaviest to the lightest, with the difference being statistically significant or close to significant for novels and comics. The groups were equally enthusiastic about reading poetry, and comparisons were more enthusiastic about reading textbooks.*

other words, the genres Stone Soup graduates liked best were also those that the comparisons liked best. Also, variability of responses (standard deviations) was small. Both of these results indicate high stability (reliability).

Comparison with Students in Other Programs

Genres in Table 5.2 are arranged in their order of "seriousness," with classics considered the heaviest reading and picture books the lightest.

Rankings by both groups tend to decline in Table 5.2 as they move from heavier to lighter reading.

Overall, Stone Soup graduates were more enthusiastic about reading for all genres combined; their average score was 0.11 points more positive than comparisons, on a three-point scale.

Discussion

Graduates of an elementary school that strongly encouraged self-selected pleasure reading did not show a bias toward lighter reading, as compared to children in a traditional program. In fact, they showed more interest toward reading in general.

This is an encouraging result, but the difference between the two groups was not large. Also, neither group appeared to be truly excited about reading, with both groups averaging about 2.0 on a 1–3 scale, "somewhat interested" in reading. This result, however, might not accurately reflect their attitudes, as we discuss below.

The junior high students who were interviewed, Stone Soup graduates and others, advised us that their schools did not have a school library. Research in English-speaking countries consistently shows that the school library is an important source of reading material (Krashen, 2004). The lack of a school library, as well as heavy academic demands placed on the students, could have influenced attitudes about reading.

Results for two of the genres were problematic and suggest that in these cases students were not being completely truthful about their reading tastes. We discuss these problems in the next section.

Comics

The respondents said that they were not especially interested in comic books, averaging slightly less than "somewhat interested" in their responses, a result not fully in agreement with other studies as well as with our observations.

☐ *Compared to traditional students, Stone Soup graduates were more interested in reading novels and comics, and less interested in reading textbooks on their own.*

Ujiie and Krashen (1996) asked American seventh-graders if they were "heavy," "occasional," or non–comic book readers. Assuming that heavy=1, occasional=2, and non=3 in this study, it is possible to compare these results to the Stone Soup results (Table 5.3). Both middle-class and lower socioeconomic status (SES) American seventh-graders are somewhat more interested in comic books than Hefei seventh-graders.

Table 5.3: Interest in Comic Books

US low SES	1.72
US middle class	1.84
Stone Soup	2.08
Comparison	2.29

Sixty-five percent of American sixth-graders studied by Worthy, Moorman, and Turner (1999) said they would read "cartoons and comics" often, ranking them second among reading preferences. Fifty-one percent of the American sixth-graders questioned by Ivy and Broaddus (2001) said they "liked to read" comic books.

Our observations indicate that despite the Stone Soup students' responses, comic books were quite popular. According to our conversations with the students, teachers, librarians, and the two volunteers who worked with us, students were avid comic book readers. This was also confirmed by our observations of activity at the convenience stores located near each school. Comics were displayed at a prominent place in the stores, and students were clearly very interested in them.

A likely explanation for the students' unenthusiastic responses to comic books on our questionnaire is that students feel that the school and their parents do not value comic book reading. There were, for example, no comic books in the library we observed in a Stone Soup elementary school. In contrast, we have observed that the comic section in bookstores in China is always packed with eager children. One does not see this level of interest in any other section of the bookstore.

☐ *We suspect that students liked reading comic books more than they admitted.*

This could provide the basis for additional research: *What children say they read* vs. *What they really read*.

Textbooks

Enthusiasm for voluntary reading of textbooks was surprisingly high. We find it very hard to believe that textbook reading was so popular. Our survey question made it very clear that we were investigating free choice reading. Either the textbooks used in these schools were unusually fascinating, or students were telling us what they thought we wanted to hear, as may have been the case with comic book reading. Do children gather around the textbook section in bookstores or in the school library?

☐ *We suspect that students liked reading textbooks less than they said they did.*

Picture Books

The Stone Soup schools place a great deal of emphasis on picture books in the early years of school, which explains the finding that the Stone Soup students liked picture books more than comparisons did, but the low ranking for picture books in general is no surprise: Picture books are aimed at younger students, and our subjects were seventh-graders. Similarly, only 16% of the sixth-graders studied in Worthy et al. (1999) said they would read picture books "often."

Gender

A possible problem with this study is that the date were not analyzed in terms of gender. Boys and girls clearly have different interests and different genre preferences; for example, boys have been reported to be more interested in comic books than girls are (Krashen, 2004).

Conclusion

The results suggest that fears that allowing self-selected reading will result in an avoidance of "serious" literature are unfounded: Stone Soup graduates were more enthusiastic about classics (but the difference was not statistically significant) and novels (close to significant), and were just as interested in poetry as comparisons, a result consistent with studies showing that children who do self-selected reading eventually choose what experts have decided are "good books" (Schoonover, 1938).

The Complexity Study: Do They Read Only "Easy" Books?

6

Will children read more books and more difficult or complex books as they progress to higher grades, given an ample supply of books, the freedom to choose their own books, and encouragement to read outside of school?

The Problem

Most adults, teachers, and schools insist that children be "required" to read certain books. They are concerned that children, supplied with an abundance of reading materials and encouraged to read for pleasure, will stay with easy books, and not move on to more challenging reading. This study was designed to determine if this concern is justified.

It can be argued that there is nothing wrong with reading "easy" books. So-called "easy reading" can contain language at or over the student's level: the reading level of a book is an average. It can also provide background knowledge, which will make other reading more comprehensible and stimulate more interest in reading.

Even if easy reading were a waste of time, the available evidence strongly suggests that children don't do much of it.

Southgate, Arnold, and Johnson (1981) reported that books children select on their own are often more difficult than the reading material assigned by teachers. Shin and Krashen (2007) noted that sixth-grade children who were reading below grade level and who were enrolled in a summer reading program selected books that were right for them, at about the fourth-grade level, which is exactly where they scored on the pretest given at the beginning of the summer.

The Scholastic Publishing Company recently released the results of a survey of about 1000 elementary and high school students in grades 1–12 and 500 of their parents in the United States. About half of the children had been told their reading level, and about 90 percent of these children said that they used their reading level to pick out books (p. 52). Of these children, only 7 percent said they usually picked books that were below their reading level (p. 53); 49 percent said they choose "an equal mix" of books above and below their level; 28 percent said they usually pick books above their reading level; and 16 percent usually picked books at their reading level.

Additional evidence that children do not take the path of least resistance comes from an analysis of their reading selections over time, as they mature.

LaBrant (1958) studied books selected by the same students in grades 10, 11, and 12, as part of their language arts classes. Students were not required to finish every book they selected, and were not required to report on every book they read. LaBrant reported that each year, students tended to select more complex books and selected a wider variety of genres. Narrative fiction, for example, made up 73 percent of their choices in

☐ *Previous studies show that children do not choose only "easy" books for their recreational reading. Much of what they choose is at or above their reading level.*

☐ *Young readers do not stick with "easy" books but gradually choose more demanding material to read as they get older, and expand their choice of genres.*

grade 10, but only 34 percent in grade 12. In contrast, 7 percent of their reading was drama in grade 10, and 24 percent in grade 12. La Brant concluded that the data gave "evidence of increasing reading maturity" (p. 157).

The research reported in the next sections of this chapter is, to our knowledge, the only attempt since 1958 to extend LaBrant's results: the Hefei project, a study of book selection in Chinese by Mandarin-speaking students in Hefei, China.

The Hefei Project

The data in the Hefei project came from students who had attended schools that were part of the Stone Soup Happy Reading Alliance (SSHRA), funded by the Hong Kong–based Chen Yet-Sen Family Foundation Limited. The SSHRA is a literacy program that focuses on developing positive attitudes toward reading in elementary school children in China. It does this by providing a great deal of time for self-selected reading (30 minutes a day), regular read-aloud sessions, full faculty involvement in reading, including the principal, who also reads aloud to children, literature circles, readers' theater, and making sure books are easy to find. In Stone Soup schools, books "are everywhere, not just in classrooms and libraries. You'll find books in corners, hallways, and lobbies. Any place is a reading place, and students are often responsible for monitoring book areas and keeping them tidy" (Gordon, 2014).

The study aimed to determine whether children read more difficult or complex books, as they move up to higher grades, when they have an ample supply of books, the freedom to choose their own books, and encouragement to read outside of school.

Procedure

Participants

□ *The goal of this study: to see whether students in China in a program that encouraged self-selected reading choose more demanding reading material as they mature.*

Fourteen children, in the seventh grade in the 48th high school in Hefei (安徽合肥), Anhui Province, China, constituted the focus group for this study. They had studied at an elementary school that had been supported by the Chen Yet-Sen Family Foundation Limited (see Chapter 5 for details of this program). Borrowing records from the school library for the past three years provided the data used in this study.

Data Collection

Three types of data were collected from children's borrowing records from third through sixth grade:

1. The number of books each child read in each semester for five semesters

2. The total number of words in each book for all books read by each child

3. The difficulty level of the content, for example, the main message, morale, or ideology delivered in the book

Information necessary to determine the number of books read and the total number of words read (1 and 2 above) was available from the automated library management system. For (3), the difficulty level of the books, a special procedure was developed that involved substantial discussion among the researchers, followed by discussion among five teachers experienced in teaching language arts.

Book Evaluation

The book evaluation was done in two steps. The first step took place in Taiwan and involved the four members of the research team (three master's-level assistants and the lead researcher), who all read the same five books and rated each book's difficulty, focusing on two aspects of the book: language and content. For each book, raters assigned a score for the two aspects, from 1, the easiest, to 9, the most complex. Then the raters met and discussed the reasons they assigned a certain score in order to reach an agreement on the ratings. This procedure resulted in a single score (the average of the scores for language and content) representing the overall difficulty level of each book. The purpose of this stage of the evaluation was to determine the feasibility of the book evaluation project and to develop procedures for the second step.

□ *Experienced teachers judged the difficulty of the language and content of books the students read. In a separate analysis, students rated the difficulty of the books.*

The second step of the evaluation was performed in Hefei. The process was as follows:

1. Five experienced elementary school teachers met in the school library and examined each book, without knowing when the book had been read during the three years. Most of the teachers were familiar with the books because all were experienced reading teachers, and some of the books were recommended reading, especially books written by several famous and popular writers of children's literature (e.g., Wu Meichen 伍美珍, Cao Wenxuan 曹文軒). The teachers examined the book covers, read the introductions, and browsed through the books, identifying sample texts that helped them arrive at a complexity score for each book, using the nine-point scheme developed in step 1, as described above.

2. In order to reach agreement, the teachers negotiated with one another, presenting their own reasons for assigning the scores they did.

3. After all teachers agreed on ratings, one or two of the most difficult or complex books read in each semester by each child were selected. This resulted in 12 piles (two piles per semester) of 8 to 10 books.

4. From these piles, the path of reading levels was drawn, showing whether children improved, regressed, or stayed at their comfort zone from third through sixth grades (Figures 6.1 to 6.5).

The teachers involved in this book evaluation task had considerable teaching experience, ranging from 3 to 24 years; they knew the books well and constantly recommended books for children to read. During the evaluation process, the teachers enthusiastically discussed each book, demonstrating their rich knowledge of children's literature.

Students as Raters

We then attempted to determine whether the students perceive book difficulty in the same way as adults do. Five older students (grades 5 and 6) were invited to rank the difficulty level of the same texts the teachers evaluated. They were asked to rank each pile of books from the easiest to the hardest.

Because of the students' limited time and energy, we decided to ask each student evaluator to rate books read by only one reader—there was no discussion among the raters. The child raters were asked to browse through the books and to read a few pages, and then order the books according to difficulty instead of assigning a score for each book.

Results

As noted ealier, we included several different measures of progress: the number of books borrowed, the number of words contained in the books, and teacher judgments of language and content complexity.

Number of Books and Words Read

Tables 6.1a and 6.1b show the numbers of words and books borrowed from the library by the 12 readers for seven semesters, from the first semester of grade 3 to the first semester of grade 6.

Unfortunately, the library management system did not provide complete data for all readers. Also, grade 6 data for the second semester were not available. Nevertheless, the data we had were sufficient to show a clear pattern of progress for these students in terms of the quantity read through the semesters.

☐ *As children get older, they read more, but the path is not a simple linear path.*

Table 6.1a: Number of Books Read

Name/Grade	3(1)	3(2)	4(1)	4(2)	5(1)	5(2)	6(1)	Total
Fong, JW	6	6	10	9	8	8	10	57
Wang, SQ	6	6	10	10	8	10	19	69
Ran, YH	0	6	10	10	8	10	10	54
Wang, YY	6	6	5	5	6	7	0	35
Yeh, YB	5	6	5	8	6	5	10	43
Wang, XY	6	6	10	10	8	10	10	60
Chen, XY	3	4	4	7	8	9	9	44
Zheng, HT	6	6	9	10	8	9	10	58
Wu, RC	6	6	5	0	8	0	8	33
Tang, WH	5	6	9	0	8	10	10	48
Ji, DY	6	6	10	10	8	10	10	60
Huang, YH	6	6	10	10	8	10	10	60

Table 6.1b: Number of Words Read

Name/ Grades	3(1)	3(2)	4(1)	4(2)	5(1)	5(2)	6(1)	Total
Fong, JW	17	18	92	125	68	73	151	393
Wang, SQ	111	218	268	259	190.9	128	373	1174.9
Ran, YY	0	49	84	40.9	186.3	111	213	471.2
Wang, YY	31	58	51	59.7	95.95	81	0	376.65
Yeh, YB	24	45	180	170	125.8	61	327	605.8
Wang, XY	41	43	51	41	60	145	105	381
Chen, XY	34	18	52	70	175	245	157	594
Zheng, HT	28	26	361	575	102.9	665	704	1757.9
Tang, WH	39	40	95	0	75	132	277	759
Ji, DY	20	38	552	265	414	418	223	1707
Huang, YH	29	42	64	75	70	86	138	366

Note: Each unit = 10,000 words.

There was, however, some variation: the following three figures show how children varied in the number of words they read for each semester (Figures 6.1 to 6.3). These figures suggest that children follow their own path, some reading more or less depending on their interests and how much

Figure 6.1: The numbers of words read

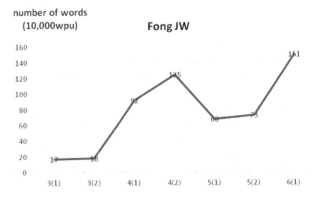

Figure 6.2: Number of words read

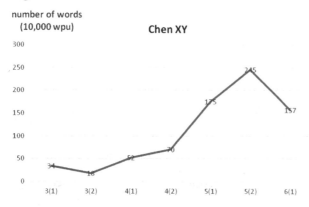

Figure 6.3: Number of words read

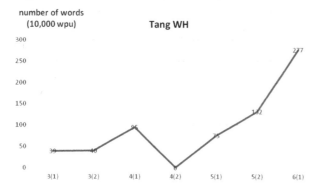

time they have. Eventually, as long as they keep reading, nearly all children will have read considerably more by the time they reach higher grade levels.

Students read a mean of about 38,000 words during the first semester of the time period under consideration, and read much more during the last semester (mean ~ 195,000). This difference was, of course, statistically significant—in other words, it is highly unlikely that it could have happened by chance. Data were available for only seven of the eight semesters.[1]

Books Read

Visual inspection of Table 6.1 shows that using books read as a measure of progress gives results similar to those obtained using words read. This was confirmed statistically: students read a mean of 5.21 books during the first semester of the period under consideration (first semester, grade 3), and read significantly more (mean = 9.71) during the last semester (first semester, grade 6). This difference was highly significant and unlikely to have occurred by chance.[2]

Number of books read is, of course, a crude measure, as some books are very short and others long; the previous measure, number of words read, is more sensitive. But neither measure can really reflect the true difficulty level of a book, the depth of description, the intricacies of the plot, and the motivations of the characters' actions. For this reason, our analysis includes expert judgments, presented in the next sections.

Complexity

As previously mentioned, the teachers evaluated the books using a nine-point scale developed by the research team, whereas the student evaluators were asked only to place the books in order of their perceived level of difficulty. For each student reader, teacher evaluators picked one to three books with the highest scores on the complexity scale; thus, about 9 to 13 books were compiled for each reader. Table 6.2 presents the 13 books read by one student, Fong, and the results of evaluations by the child and teacher evaluators.

Table 6.2: Books Read by Fong

Grade	Book Title	Order (Child)	Score (Teacher)	Book Title	Order (Child)	Score (Teacher)
1st, grade 3	兒童文學	1	4	窗邊的小豆豆	6	5
2nd, grade 3	感恩的故事	8	5			
1st, grade 4	烏丟丟奇遇記	7	5	小飛俠彼得潘	10	7
2nd, grade 4	青銅葵花	5	7	狼王洛波	2	7
1st, grade 5	威斯汀遊戲	12	7	不老泉	9	8
2nd, grade 5	上下五千年	11	7	絕響	3	9
1st, grade 6	簡愛	4	9	蘇菲的世界	13	9

The teacher evaluation results in Figure 6.4 reveal that Fong read increasingly difficult books as she progressed to higher grades levels. The student evaluator, placing the books in their perceived order of difficulty, produced a less linear trend then the teachers did, but there is still a clear increase in complexity over time. The student valuation order and the teachers' order agreed with each other closely.[3]

□ *As children got older, the books they read were more demanding, according to both teacher and student ratings.*

Figure 6.4: Evaluation results for Fong JW

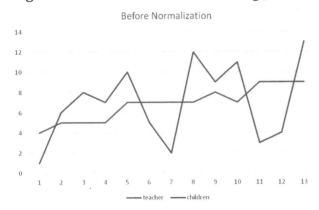

Before Normalization

— teacher — children

The pattern becomes even more salient when normalized to make the two evaluation results comparable, for example, making 9 the maximum score for both child and teacher evaluations (see the dotted line in Figure 6.5).

Figure 6.5: The pattern of progress for Fong JW, after normalization

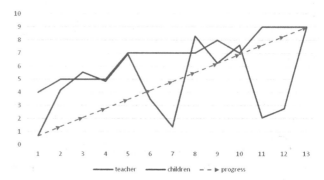

The second case, RQ Wu, shows that the child evaluation was very consistent with the teacher evaluation. Both evaluation results show that Wu read books that increased in level of complexity (Figure 6.6), and the child evaluation order agreed closely with the teachers' order.[4]

Figure 6.6. The pattern of progress for Wu Run Qiu.

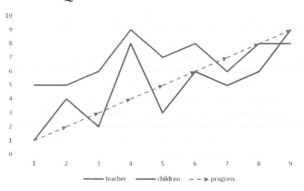

Summary and Conclusions

As children mature, they read more: this was shown by both a count of the total number of words read as well as the total number of books read. In addition, the complexity of the books they read, as judged by both teachers and students, increased.

These results are consistent with those of LaBrant (1958), described earlier, who showed high school students in the United States gradually expand the kinds of reading they do as they mature, moving into a wider variety of and more complex genres.

In the previous chapter, it was shown that those who graduate from programs that encourage self-selected reading do not avoid literature of high quality. In this chapter, the data are also reassuring: Children in a print-rich environment in which they are free to select their own reading do not stay with easy books. They not only read more as they mature, but they also select, on their own, books that are harder to read and have more complicated plots.

Notes

1. For those interested in the statistical details: Application of a *t*-test for correlated samples showed that the difference between words read during the first and last semester of reading to be highly significant: $t=3.01$, $df=5$; $p=0.015$, one tail.

2. Application of a *t*-test for correlated samples showed the difference between books read during and the first and last semester to be highly significant, $t=4.07$, $df=13$, $t<0.001$, one tail.

3. Correlation between the student evaluation order and the teachers' order: rho=0.75, $p=0.0034$.

4. Correlation between the student evaluation order and the teachers' order: rho=0.84, $p=0.005$.

What Have We Learned from PIRLS?

7

In this chapter, we present additional evidence confirming the importance of access to compelling comprehensible input—namely, libraries—and also present important evidence that strongly suggests that access to libraries can balance, or at least reduce, the devastating negative impact of poverty on reading achievement. Our source is a well-known international test: the PIRLS test.

The PIRLS Test

PIRLS (Progress in International Reading Literacy Study) regularly administers a reading test to fourth-graders in over 40 countries. The PIRLS test attempts to measure both reading for literary experience and reading to acquire and use information (Mullis, Martin, Kennedy, and Foy, 2007). Students take the test in their national language.

PIRLS provides not only test scores but also the results of an extensive questionnaire given to teachers, parents, and students, which includes questions concerning attitudes, reading behavior outside of school, and classroom practices (Mullis et al., 2007). PIRLS also supplies data on socioeconomic status.

Krashen, Lee, and McQuillan (2012) presented two analyses of the PIRLS test administered in 2006. Both analyses covered the countries

☐ *The PIRLS test is a reading test given to 10-year-olds in over 40 countries, in their first language.*

for which complete data were available for all variables under study.

The study reported here attempts to replicate one of these analyses, the "simple" analysis that only included a few selected variables. The other analysis reported by Krashen, Lee, and McQuillan (2012) analyzed all data supplied by PIRLS and then entered the factors into a multiple regression. Both analyses yielded similar results.

In the simple analysis, a single predictor was chosen to represent each factor. The predictor in each case was felt to be most representative of the factor Krashen et al. were interested in investigating.

A widely used measure, the Human Development Index (HDI) developed by the United Nations (UN), was used to represent **socioeconomic status (SES)**. The Human Development Index is an average of three factors: education (adult literacy rates, school enrollment), life expectancy, and wealth (logarithm of income: see http://hdr.undp.org/en/content/human-development-index-hdi). The UN considers a high HDI rating to be between 0.8 and 0.95; a mid rating to be between 0.5 and 0.79; and a low rating to be between 0.34 and 0.49.

In addition to the HDI, the analysis included several other predictors:

> **independent reading**—the percentage of students in each country who read independently in school every day or almost every day.

> **library**—represented by the percentage of school libraries in each country with over 500 books.

> **instruction**—the average hours per week devoted to reading instruction in each country.

☐ *The study reported here compared the impact of poverty, independent reading, the availability of a school library, and direct instruction on PIRLS test scores.*

70

Table 7.1 presents the results of a multiple regression analysis, a procedure that allows us to examine the impact of each of the predictors uninfluenced by the other predictors. For example, there is a positive correlation between SES (HDI) and the availability of school libraries with at least 500 books: Countries with higher SES levels have a higher percentage of schools with well-equipped libraries ($r=0.37$; appendix, Krashen et al., 2012). Multiple regression tells us the impact of school libraries controlling for the effect of SES, as if SES and library access were unrelated.

According to Table 7.1, SES has the strongest effect on reading scores, as reflected by the value of the beta associated with SES (beta=0.41), a result consistent with nearly all studies examining the impact of poverty on literacy development. Independent reading was also positively associated with reading scores, in agreement with numerous studies showing the value of in-school reading, that is, sustained silent reading (Krashen, 2004), but the beta size fell just short of statistical significance.

The effect of independent reading was not as large as the effect of SES (beta=0.16, compared to beta=0.41).

□ *Previous studies consistently show that high poverty is related to lower reading scores. This study found the same result.*

Table 7.1: Predictors of the Reading Test: PIRLS 2006

Predictor	Beta	p
SES	0.41	0.005
Independent reading	0.16	0.14
Library: 500 books	0.35	0.005
Instruction	−0.19	0.085

$r^2=0.63$

The percentage of students who had access to a library of at least 500 books ("Library" in

Table 7.1) was positively related to reading scores, and the beta was large, nearly as large as the effect of SES. This is a very important result because it suggests that providing access to a library can balance the negative effect of poverty. This makes sense: access to books results in more recreational reading, and recreational reading results in better literacy development (Krashen, 2004). Children of poverty lack access to books; good libraries provide this access, which results in more reading and better literacy development.

☐ Previous studies consistently show that availability of a library is related to higher reading scores. This study found the same result.

The final predictor, the amount of literacy instruction, was negatively related to reading scores. Those in schools providing more reading instruction had lower scores on the PIRLS examination, even when SES was controlled. This result may seem surprising, but it is consistent with other research. "Reading instruction" nearly always means direct instruction in the elements of literacy, such as phonemic awareness and phonics. There is no demonstrated relationship between instruction in phonemic awareness and tests of reading comprehension (Krashen, 2001), and it has been demonstrated that "intensive, systematic phonics" instruction only helps children do better on tests in which they pronounce words presented in isolation; it does not contribute to performance on tests of reading comprehension (Garan, 2002; Krashen, 2009).

☐ Previous studies consistently show that direct instruction is not related to higher reading scores. This study found the same result.

Table 7.1 indicates that $r^2 = 0.63$. This indicates that the combined, the four predictors in this table provide 63 percent of the information needed to predict a country's PIRLS score. This is a very high percentage.

Replication of the Simple Analysis, Based on PIRLS, 2011

A similar analysis was performed on data from PIRLS 2011. Following Krashen, Lee, and McQuillan (2012), the United Nations HDI was used as a measure of SES (Human Development Report, Summary, 2011 (http://hdr.undp.org/en /content/human-development-index-hdi).

> *Library* in the 2011 PIRLS is defined as the percentage of students in each country who had access to a school library containing at least 5,000 books. In our previous study of PIRLS predictors, the school library, defined as the percentage of students in each country who had access to a school library containing at least 500 books, was a strong predictor of PIRLS reading sores (Krashen, Lee, and McQuillan, 2012), even when SES (HDI) was controlled.

> *Instruction* is defined as the total number of hours per year dedicated to reading instruction, including reading across the curriculum (both in and outside of reading class) (PIRLS 2011, Exhibit 8.4).

In the analysis of PIRLS 2006, we included the percentage of students who were given time for independent reading in school. This question was not asked in the 2011 PIRLS.

Additional Predictors

This replication included a number of additional predictors not included in the analysis of PIRLS 2006. One of these additional predictors was a book access variable, called *"Classroom library"* (abbreviated as Classlibr), included to supplement the analysis of the school library:

"Classroom library" is defined as the percentage of students with access to a classroom library containing at least 50 books.

The impact of parents' reading habits was also included: *"Parental reading"* (parent read) was defined as the percentage of parents in each country who say they like to read.

In addition, *"Early literacy achievement"* (early lit) was included because of the common view that reading development can be improved if we prepare young children for school with early (preschool) direct reading instruction. Early literacy achievement was defined by PIRLS as the percentage of parents who report that their child could perform three of the following five tasks "very well" and two others at least "moderately well."

1. Recognize most of the letters of the alphabet.

2. Read some words.

3. Read sentences.

4. Write letters of the alphabet.

5. Write some words.

Table 7.2 presents the multiple regression analysis:

Table 7.2: Replication: PIRLS 2011

Predictor	Beta	p
SES	0.52	0.01
Library: 5,000 books	0.2	0.08
Class library	0.08	0.28
Parent read	0.065	0.31
Early lit	−0.26	0.04
Instruction	−0.016	0.5

$r^2 = 0.62$.

Once again, SES is the strongest predictor, with the largest beta. And once again, access to a school library is a substantial predictor, falling just short of statistical significance. It is not as large as it was in the original study, but is still impressive.

Classroom libraries and parental reading habits were not significant predictors of reading scores. Both of these variables correlated positively with PIRLS reading scores (classroom libraries and reading scores, $r=0.34$; parental reading and reading scores, $r=0.39$), but both were also correlated with SES (classroom libraries and SES; $r=0.35$; parental reading and SES; $r=0.56$). When SES is taken into consideration, or "controlled," the relationship between classroom libraries and reading scores and the relationship between parental reading and reading scores disappears.

□ *Contrary to popular opinion, classroom libraries and parents' reading habits were not related to reading scores when poverty level is included in the analysis.*

As was the case in the 2006 analysis, time dedicated to reading instruction was not related to reading proficiency. Unlike the earlier analysis, however, the relationship was not negative, but nearly zero.

The relationship between early literacy achievement—that is, parents' judgment of the child's literacy skill on entering school—and reading ability measured five years later was significantly negative. The simple correlation between early literacy achievement and PIRLS test scores was negative and significant ($r=-0.33$) and remained negative and significant in the multiple regression analysis.

□ *The child's early mastery of "literacy skills" (letters of alphabet, early writing) does not predict later reading ability.*

Summary

In both the original study and the replication study, SES was a powerful predictor. In both studies, access to a school library was a positive predictor of reading scores, even when controlling for

SES. In one study, the size of the impact was large; in the other it was modest. Other studies have produced similar results (reviewed in Krashen, 2011c; a recent contribution to this research is Adkins, 2015).

None of the other predictors were significant when SES was controlled. The positive relationship seen between parents' reading habits and reading scores, as well as classroom libraries and reading scores, was, in this study, an artifact of their positive relationship with SES. Children of parents who read more do indeed read better, but parental reading is not the cause of the children's better reading achievement. Children with access to better classroom libraries also read better, but the classroom library is not the cause, admittedly an unusual result.

Some Special Cases: Hong Kong and Taiwan

Table 7.3 presents average (mean) scores on the PIRLS 2011 for Hong Kong and Taiwan.

Table 7.3: Mean Scores on PIRLS 2011

	Mean	Sd	HK	Taiwan
Score	507.6	55.4	571	553
HDI	0.82	0.087	0.9	0.88
Library: 5,000 books	30.34	26.7	82	90
Class library	25.2	20.3	75	73
Parent read	31.11	11.15	14	17
Early lit	26.3	11.7	41	30
Instruction	143.34	42.05	102	65

Both Hong Kong and Taiwan are very high scoring countries on the PIRLS. Hong Kong, in fact, ranked number one in the world, and the

Taiwan average was a full standard deviation above the mean for all countries tested.

Both Hong Kong and Taiwan also score extremely high on school libraries and classroom libraries, and our analysis suggested that the school library quality is the crucial one.

Parents in both Hong Kong and Taiwan reported reading less than average for all countries tested. According to our analysis, however, parental reading is not a significant factor in producing higher reading scores.

Both Hong Kong and Taiwan do better than average in "early literacy," but in our analysis, a higher performance in early literacy was associated with lower reading on the PIRLS. Both countries were well below the average in total time dedicated to reading instruction, but according to both analyses above, time dedicated to reading instruction is not a significant predictor of reading achievement, and in the 2006 analysis, it was negatively related to reading achievement.

Some Disturbing Data

There is an additional factor particular to Hong Kong, Taiwan, and two other countries (Italy and Singapore). According to questionnaire results from PIRLS 2011, neither children nor adults (their parents) in these countries report reading much. Table 7.4 compares the percentage who say they "like reading" in these countries with "baseline" countries, other countries with high socioeconomic status and high PIRLS scores (Loh and Krashen, 2015).

□ *Some countries appear to be "test prep" countries: those with high reading scores, but with little interest in reading among children or adults.*

One suspects that the high PIRLS scores achieved by these countries are not achieved in the normal way, via self-selected reading of interesting books (see Chapter 4). A troubling possibility is

Table 7.4: Interest in Reading, HDI (SES), and PIRLS Scores

Country	HDI	Parent Likes	Child Likes	PIRLS
Hong Kong	0.90	14	21	571
Taiwan	0.88	17	23	553
Italy	0.87	24	23	541
Singapore	0.87	21	22	567
MEANS	0.88 (0.01)	19 (4.4)	22.3 (0.96)	558 (13.7)
Baseline	.91 (.01)	43.7 (5.2)	33 (2.5)	538.4 (9.7)

that the high scores are a result of massive required reading, test preparation, and teaching strategies that increase scores without increasing competence, for example, teaching children which questions to skip, when to guess and when not to, and so forth. The PIRLS data suggest that this approach fails to result in enthusiasm for reading, thereby preventing the continuing development of literacy.

Excluded Variables

Many factors that could play important roles in literacy development were not included in this analysis, including reading aloud to students when they were younger (although PIRLS included reading aloud as part of a broader variable) and access to public libraries.

Books in the home (percentage of students who live in homes with at least 100 books) was included by PIRLS, but inclusion in the analysis resulted in multicollinearity (extremely high correlation with other predictors). A simple analysis, however, revealed that although books in the home correlated with PIRLS scores ($r=0.59$), it was also very highly correlated with SES ($r=0.81$), and a small-scale multiple regression analysis confirmed that when SES is controlled, books in the home has no effect on reading scores (Table 7.5). Hong Kong and Taiwan were close to the international mean for this variable, with Taiwan slightly above.

Table 7.5: Impact of Books in the Home, with SES Controlled

	Beta	p
HDI	0.73	0
Books in home	0.023	0.46

$r^2 = 0.49$.

As was the case with parental reading and classroom libraries, it appears that the relationship between reading achievement and the home print environment is the result of the influence of SES.

□ *Do more books in the home mean better reading? The research does not yet give a clear answer.*

We are hesitant to ignore this variable, however, as there is some evidence suggesting that when SES is controlled, books in the home might be a predictor of literacy development. In one study, for example, middle-class (high school) students coming from homes with a more print-rich environment (books owned, magazine subscriptions) engage in more free voluntary reading in their first language (Chinese) (Lee and Krashen, 1996). In another study, focusing on fourth-graders in Hong Kong, "family reading financial capital," which included the child's estimate of the number of books in the home and parents' average expense on buying books, was a significant predictor of reading proficiency, controlling for several SES predictors: father's education and employment, and family financial status (Tse, Lam, Ip, Loh, and Tso, 2010).

Motivation to read was not included in the analysis because it was based on questions that lacked validity. Some of the questions were clearly related to extrinsic motivation, (e.g., "It is important to be a good reader"; "My parents like it when I read"; "I need to read well for my future"; etc.) and, oddly, none of the questions related to reading enjoyment.

Conclusions

☐ *The major conclusions: Poverty is related to lower reading achievement. Libraries are related to higher reading achievement.*

Some countries achieve higher scores on international reading tests than others. The major reasons, according to our analysis, are poverty and lack of access to reading materials in school libraries.[1] These results make sense: a number of studies confirm that poverty has a devastating impact on school performance: Children who live in poverty often suffer from food deprivation and lack of health care (Berliner, 2009), as well as a lack access to books in their homes, neighborhoods and in their schools (Krashen, 1997).

Our results are also in agreement with research on the positive impact of libraries. Research consistently tells us that better libraries mean higher reading scores (see McQuillan, 1998, and studies reviewed in Krashen, 2004). Keith Curry Lance's school library impact studies provide strong evidence that confirms the positive impact of school library quality and library staffing on reading achievement. (For extensive reports, see, for example, http://keithcurrylance.com/school-library-imp act-studies/).

Both analyses presented here suggest that a good school library can compensate for some of the effects of poverty by providing access to reading material. But in light of the "disturbing results" presented earlier, it is to be determined whether children in some countries actually take advantage of greater access to books, whether at home or in libraries.

The amount of direct instruction in school in reading was not related to reading achievement, nor was "early literacy achievement," represented by parents' report of literacy competence on entering school. Both of these results are consistent with studies showing a lack of impact of phonemic awareness and intensive phonics on tests of reading comprehension (Krashen, 2001; Garan, 2002; Krashen, 2009), and are consistent with the hypothesis that our proficiency in phonics and spelling is the result of reading, not instruction (Smith, 2004; Krashen, 2004).

An important result of our second analysis is that two factors, parental reading and classroom libraries, commonly thought to be important to literacy development in children, may not be, but are, rather, the result of the presence or lack of poverty. This appears to be the case for books in the home, but other results make us hesitant to discard this source of books.

What is clear is that poverty is the main factor affecting school performance. This is nothing new in the education research, but is unrecognized in most discussions of school policy. Here is a notable exception:

> We are likely to find that the problems of housing and education, instead of preceding the elimination of poverty, will themselves be affected if poverty is first abolished. (Martin Luther King, 1967)

Note

1. Adkins (2014) reported that the presence of a school library did not predict math, reading, or English achievement for American 15-year-olds who took the PISA exam in 2009, but nearly all schools in her sample were in the United States and had a library. "Library adequacy," based on

principals' judgment of the adequacy of the library staff and materials, was, however, positively associated with scores in math, reading, and science, controlling for the effect of poverty. Technological adequacy of the library was a negative predictor of test scores. This was, however, not the case for students in the lowest levels of achievement.

Adkins's findings on principals' perception of library adequacy can be interpreted as parallel to ours: access to a library counts, even when social class is controlled, and the library plays some role in balancing the effect of poverty.

Thus, in countries where libraries are nearly universal, presence or absence of a library will not be related to academic achievement. But library quality does make a difference.

	Math	Reading	Science
Predictors	Beta	Beta	Beta
Wealth	0.705*	0.722*	0.632*
Library	−0.072	−0.193*	−0.212*
Library adequacy	0.212*	0.158*	0.226*
Tech adequacy	−0.157	−0.16*	−0.174*
r^2	0.57	0.625	0.542

Source: Adkins, 2014.

Conclusions

We have spent seven chapters focused on one central idea: compelling comprehensible input (CCI). We have presented evidence that CCI is the key to language and literacy development and have suggested that CCI means the end of traditional ideas about motivation for reading (Chapter 1).

We have described the three stages readers go through in developing the highest levels of literacy, all involving CCI (Chapters 2, 3, and 4), and have provided evidence that readers, when allowed and enabled to select their own reading, do not stick to substandard texts, but rather select more demanding reading material as they mature (Chapter 6).

Our interpretation of the PIRLS results is that making compelling reading available in libraries contributes to literacy development, whereas activities that do not provide CCI, such as reading instruction in school and the development of early literacy skills, do not contribute to literacy development (Chapter 7).

☐ Our conclusions: read to children and focus on the story; provide access to interesting reading; give students time to read; and allow them to self-select their own reading material.

The pedagogical implications, we think, are obvious. The essential ones are to read to young children with a focus on the story, not the details of the written text; to provide access to interesting reading material; and to give students time to read.

CCI may, however, have wider implications.

CCI and the Goals of Education

□ Schools need to prepare students for an uncertain future, not for what is needed right now. Things change.

We argue here that it is impossible for society to make detailed plans for the future: CCI helps make sure that today's students and society will be prepared for whatever might come. A popular view is that we must prepare today's students for what some people call "21st Century Skills." Many "experts" behave as if they know what these skills are. Most of us have no idea.

The history of science and technology has taught us that new developments are nearly always a surprise. One of the "experts," former US Secretary of Education Arne Duncan, expressed this idea a few years ago in an interview with *USA Today*:

> As we get more and more of these technological breakthroughs, there are going to be jobs in fields available that don't even exist today. If these guys [sic] can come out and be those innovators and be those creators and inventors, they're going to create new opportunities that we can't even envision or begin to comprehend today (Toppo, Vergano, and USA Today, 2009).

This uncertainty still reigns.

The only way to prepare students for the future is to avoid premature specialization, based on society's perceived current needs. Rather, we should make sure that students are prepared to take advantage of options that may not be obvious right now—or that may not even exist.

Preparing for Change: Pursue Your Strengths

Zhao (2009) arrives at the same conclusion and adds an important point: School should help students "pursue their strengths":

... it is ... *difficult to predict what new businesses will emerge and what will become obsolete. Thus, what becomes highly valuable are unique talents, knowledge, and skills, the ability to adapt to changes, and creativity, all of which calls for a school culture that respects and cultivates expertise in a diversity of talents and skills and a curriculum that enables individuals to pursue their strengths* (Zhao, 2009, p. 156).

☐ *The best way to prepare for an uncertain future: Pursue your strengths and specialize.*

Don't Worry about Going to Your Left

We do not allow students to pursue their strengths very much. Instead, we force all students to reach demanding levels in what some people consider to be "basics" before they can specialize. This is not a good idea.

Rosenblatt (2001) advises young basketball players not to worry so much about learning to go to their left, their weak direction: if you are always working on weak areas, you can never really excel at anything.

It is undeniable that all citizens need a certain minimum competence in some crucial areas, such as reading and math, but not nearly as much as is often thought to be required. Nor is it necessary to hurry development of weaker areas while delaying involvement in areas of real interest. There is much too much delayed gratification in education today, resulting often in students leaving the system before they have a chance to discover and "pursue their strengths," and the current worldwide standards movement promises to exacerbate this problem.

A major responsibility of school is to provide the means for students to explore their interests and develop their talents so they can reach their full potential. This means broadening curriculum options rather than making them narrower

(Ohanian, 1999, p. 4; Zhao, 1999, p. 181–83; Tudball, 2010).

Kurt Vonnegut may be right: "[W]e shouldn't be seeking harrowing challenges, but rather tasks we find natural and interesting, tasks we were apparently born to perform" (Vonnegut, 1997, p. 148). The teacher's job is to help students find those tasks they love to do and that they can learn to do very well, and that excellence will contribute to society.

The Role of Compelling Reading

□ *Self-selected reading helps readers discover their interests and can help them develop competence to follow their interests.*

Compelling reading is an important part of helping students discover their interests and their strengths. Self-selected, compelling reading has played an important role in the lives of many highly successful people. Simonton (1988) summarized a number of studies of the development of creativity and concluded that "omnivorous reading in childhood and adolescence correlates positively with ultimate adult success" (Simonton, 1988, p. 11).

There is good reason for this: as we noted earlier (Chapter 4), as readers develop more competence in literacy, they also learn more about a wide range of topics. Much of this occurs during what we have called stage 2, when readers are often largely reading fiction.

Emery and Csikszentmihalyi (1982) compared 15 men of blue-collar background who became college professors with 15 men of very similar background who grew up to become blue-collar workers. The future professors lived in a much more print-rich environment and did far more reading when they were young. They thus had a better chance of finding what, for them, was compelling, and discovering their interests, in addition to building literacy and knowledge.

A good example of the impact of reading is Malcolm X, who specifically gave reading the credit for his education: "Not long ago, an English writer telephoned me from London, for the purpose of an interview. One of the questions was, 'What's your alma mater?' I told him, 'Books'" (El-Shabbaz, 1964, p. 179).

The concept of compelling comprehensible input may be one of the most crucial in all of education. It is possible that it is an important part of the path to full literacy development, full language acquisition, finding one's true interests, and developing the competence to pursue these interests.

References

Acheson, D., J. Wells, and M. MacDonald. 2008. New and updated tests of print exposure and reading abilities in college students. *Behavioral Research Methods* 40(1): 278–289.

Adkins, D. 2015. U.S. Students, Poverty, and School Libraries: What Results of the 2009 Program for International Student Assessment Tell Us. *School Library Research* 17. http://www.ala.org/aasl/slr/vol17.

Atwell, N. 2007. *The Reading Zone.* New York: Scholastic.

Bean, M. A. 1879. The evil of unlimited freedom in the use of juvenile fiction. *Library Journal*, 4: 341–43.

Berliner, D. 2009. *Poverty and Potential: Out-of-School Factors and School Success.* Boulder and Tempe: Education and the Public Interest Center & Education Policy Research Unit.

Biber, D. 1988. *Variation across Speech and Writing.* Cambridge: Cambridge University Press.

Biber, D. 2006. *University Language.* Philadelphia, PA: John Benjamins.

Blok, H. 1999. Reading to young children in educational settings: A meta-analysis of recent research. *Language Learning* 49(2): 343–371.

Brassell, D. 2003. Sixteen books went home tonight: Fifteen were introduced by the teacher. *The California Reader* 36(3): 33–39.

Bus, A., M. Van Ijzendoorn, and A. Pellegrini. 1995. Joint book reading makes for success in learning to read: A meta-analysis on intergenerational transmission of literacy. *Review of Educational Research* 65: 1–21.

Canada, G. 1995. *Fist, Stick, Knife, Gun: A Personal History of Violence.* Boston: Beacon Press.

Carlsen, G. R., and A. Sherrill. 1988. *Voices of readers: How we come to love books.* Urbana, IL: NCTE.

Carson, B. 1990. *Gifted Hands.* Grand Rapids, MI: Zondervan Books.

Cho, K. S., and Krashen, S. 1994. Acquisition of vocabulary from the Sweet Valley High Kids series: Adult ESL acquisition. *Journal of Reading* 37: 662–667.

Cho, K. S., and Krashen, S. 2015. The cure for English fever? Stories and self-selected reading in English. *KAERA Research Forum* 1(4): 41–47.

Chomsky, C. 1972. Stages in language development and reading exposure. *Harvard Educational Review* 42(1): 1–33.

Cohen, Y. 1997. How reading got me into trouble. Class paper, Trenton State University, Summer 1997.

Constantino, R., S. Y. Lee, K. S. Cho, and S. Krashen. (1997). Free voluntary reading as a predictor of TOEFL scores. *Applied Language Learning* 8: 111–118.

Csikszentmihalyi, M. 1990. *Flow: The Psychology of Optimal Experience.* New York: Harper Perennial.

Elley, W. 1991. Acquiring literacy in a second language: The effect of book-based programs. *Language Learning* 41: 375–411.

Elley, W., and F. Mangubhai. 1983. The impact of reading on second language learning. *Reading Research Quarterly* 19: 53–67.

El-Shabbaz, E. 1964. *The Autobiography of Malcolm X.* New York: Ballintine Books.

Emery, C., and M. Csikszentmihalyi. 1982. The socialization effects of cultural role models in ontogenetic development and upward mobility. *Child Psychiatry and Human Development* 12: 3–19.

Fink, R. 1995/96. Successful dyslexics: A constructivist study of passionate interest reading. *Journal of Adolescent & Adult Literacy* 39(4): 268–80.

Flurkey, A., and J. Xu, eds. 2003. *On the Revolution in Reading: The Selected Writings of Kenneth S. Goodman.* Portsmouth, NH: Heinemann.

Garan, E. 2001. Beyond the smoke and mirrors: A critique of the National Reading Panel report on phonics. *Phi Delta Kappan* 82, no. 7 (March): 500–506.

Garan, E. 2002. *Resisting Reading Mandates: How to Triumph with the Truth.* Portsmouth, NH: Heinemann.

Gardner, D. 2004. Vocabulary input through extensive reading: A comparison of words found in children's narrative and expository reading materials. *Applied Linguistics* 25(1): 1–37.

Gardner, D. 2008. Vocabulary recycling in children's authentic reading materials: A corpus-based investigation of narrow reading. *Reading as a Foreign Language*, 20(1): 92–122.

Gordon, C. 2014. A literacy lesson from China: What an exuberant culture of reading can teach us. *School Library Journal*, January, 2014.

Gradman, H., and E. Hanania. 1991. Language learning background factors and ESL proficiency. *Modern Language Journal*, 75: 39–51.

Graff, H. 1979. *The Literacy Myth: Literacy and Social Structure in the Nineteenth-Century City*. New York: Academic Press.

Hedrick, W., and J. Cunningham. 2002. Investigating the effect of wide reading on listening comprehension of written language. *Reading Psychology* 23: 107–126.

Hsieh, M. Y., F. W. Wang, and S. Y. Lee. 2011. A corpus-based analysis comparing vocabulary input from storybooks and textbooks. *The International Journal of Foreign Language Teaching* 6(1): 25–33.

Hyland, K. 1996. "I don't quite follow": Making sense of a modifier. *Language Awareness* 5(2): 91–109.

Irwin, O. 1960. Infant speech: Effect of systematic reading of stories. *Journal of Speech and Hearing Research* 3: 187–190.

Ivey, G., and K. Broaddus. 2001. "Just plain reading": A survey of what makes students want to read in middle school classrooms. *Reading Research Quarterly* 36(4): 350–377.

Justice, L. M., and H. K. Ezell. 2000. Enhancing children's print and word awareness through home-based parent intervention. *American Journal of Speech-Language Pathology* 9: 257–269.

Justice, L. M., and H. K. Ezell. 2002. Use of storybook reading to increase print awareness in at- risk children. *American Journal of Speech-Language Pathology* 11: 17–29.

Justice, L. M., J. N. Kaderavek, X. Fan, A. Sofka, and A. Hunt. 2009. Accelerating preschoolers' early literacy development through classroom-based teacher-child storybook reading and explicit print referencing. *Language, Speech, and Hearing Services in Schools* 40: 67–85.

Justice, L. M., A. McGinty, S. B. Piasta, J. N. Kaderavek, and X. Fan. 2010. Print-focused read-alouds in pre-school classrooms: Intervention effectiveness and moderators of child outcomes. *Language, Speech, and Hearing Services in Schools* 41: 504–520.

Jylha-Laide, J., and S. Karreinen. 1993. Play it again, Laura: Off-air cartoons and videos as a means of second-language learning. In K. Sajavaara and S. Takala (eds.), *Finns as Learners of English: Three Studies*. Jyväskylä: Jyväskylä Cross-Language Studies. 16: 89–145.

Kim, J., and S. Krashen. 2000. Another home run. *California English* 6(2): 25.

King, M. L. K. 1967. *Where Do We Go from Here? Chaos or Community*. New York: Harper and Row.

Knight, C., and K. Fischer. 1994. Learning to read words: Individual differences in developmental sequences. *Journal of Applied Developmental Psychology* 13: 377–404.

Krashen, S. 1982. *Principles and Practice in Second Language Acquisition*. Oxford: Pergamon Press.

Krashen, S. 1997. Bridging inequity with books. *Educational Leadership* 55(4): 18–22.

Krashen, S. 2001. Does "pure" phonemic awareness training affect reading comprehension? *Perceptual and Motor Skills* 93: 356–358.

Krashen, S. 2003. *Explorations in Language Acquisition and Use: The Taipei Lectures*. Portsmouth, NH: Heinemann.

Krashen, S. 2004. *The Power of Reading*, 2nd ed. Westport, CT: Libraries Unlimited.

Krashen, S. 2007. Extensive reading in English as a foreign language by adolescents and young adults: A meta-analysis. *International Journal of Foreign Language Teaching* 3(2): 23–29.

Krashen, S. 2009. Does intensive reading instruction contribute to reading comprehension? *Knowledge Quest* 37(4): 72–74.

Krashen, S. 2011a. Academic language proficiency: Acquired or learned? Selected papers from The Nineteenth International Symposium and

Book Fair on English Teaching. English Teachers' Association of the Republic of China, Taipei, Taiwan, November 10–14, 2010.

Krashen, S. 2011b. Reach out and read (aloud). *Language Magazine* 10(12): 17–19.

Krashen, S. 2011c. Why we should stop scolding teenagers and their schools: Frequency of leisure reading. *Language Magazine* 11(4): 18–21.

Krashen, S. 2012. Developing academic proficiency: Some hypotheses. *International Journal of Foreign Language Teaching* (2): 8–15.

Krashen, S. 2013. Read-alouds: Let's stick to the story. *Language and Language Teaching* 3, Azim Premji University and the Vidya Bhawan Society.

Krashen, S., and B. M. Mason. 2015. Can second language acquirers reach high levels of proficiency through self-selected reading? An attempt to confirm Nation's (2014) results. *International Journal of Foreign Language Teaching* 10(2): 10–19.

Krashen, S., S. Y. Lee, and J. McQuillan. 2012. Is the library important? Multivariate studies at the national and international level. *Journal of Language and Literacy Education* 8(1): 26–36.

Ku, Y.-M., and R. C. Anderson. 2001. Chinese children's incidental learning of word meanings. *Contemporary Educational Psychology* 26(2): 249–266.

LaBrant, L. 1958. An evaluation of free reading. In C. Hunnicutt and W. Iverson (eds.), *Research in the Three R's* (pp. 154–161). New York: Harper and Brothers.

Lamme, L. 1974. Authors popular among fifth graders. *Elementary English* 51: 1008–1009.

Lao, C. Y. 2003. Prospective teachers' journey to becoming readers. *New Mexico Journal of Reading* 32(2): 14–20.

Lao, C. Y., and S. Krashen. 2008. Heritage language development: Exhortation or good stories? *International Journal of Foreign Language Teaching* 4(2): 17–18.

Lao, C. Y., and S. Krashen. 2014. Language acquisition without speaking and without study. *Journal of Research of Bilingual Education Research and Instruction* 16(1): 215–221.

Layne, S. 2015. *In Defense of Read-Aloud: Sustaining Best Practice.* Portland, ME: Stenhouse.

Lee, S. Y. 1996. The relationship of free voluntary reading to writing proficiency and academic achievement among Taiwanese senior high school students. Proceedings of the Fifth International Symposium on Language Teaching (pp. 119–126). Taipei: Crane.

Lee, S. Y. 2005. Facilitating and inhibiting factors on EFL writing: A model testing with SEM. *Language Learning* 55(2): 335–374.

Lee, S. Y. 2007. Revelations from Three Consecutive Studies on Extensive Reading. *Regional Language Center (RELC) Journal* 38(2): 150–170.

Lee, S. Y., M. I. Hsieh, and F. Y. Wang. 2009. Storybooks vs. textbooks: A corpus study. Selected Papers from The Eighteenth International Symposium on English Teaching (pp. 620–624). Taipei: Crane.

Lee, S. Y. and S. Krashen. 1996. Free voluntary reading and writing competence in Taiwanese high school students. *Perceptual and Motor Skills* 83: 687–690.

Lee, M. H., S. Y. Lee, and S. Krashen. 2014. Vocabulary acquisition through read-alouds and discussion: A case study. *International Journal of Foreign Language Teaching* 9(1): 2–6.

Lin, S. Y., F. Shin, and S. Krashen. 2007. Sophia's choice: Summer reading. *Knowledge Quest* 35(4): 52–55.

Loh, E. K. Y., and S. Krashen. 2015. Patterns in PIRLS performance: The importance of liking to read, SES, and the effect of test prep. *Asian Journal of Education and e-Learning* 3(1): 1–6.

Lomax, C. 1976. Interest in books and stories at nursery school. *Educational Research* 19: 110–112.

Lonsdale, C. 2006. *The Third Ear: You Can Learn Any Language.* Hong Kong: Third Ear Books.

Martinez, M., N. Roser, J. Worthy, S. Strecker, and P. Gough. 1997. Classroom libraries and children's book selections: Redefining "access" in self-selected reading. In C. Kinzer, K. Hinchman, and D. Leu (eds.), *Inquiries in Literacy: Theory and Practice. Forty-Sixth Yearbook of The National Reading Conference* (pp. 265–272). Chicago: National Reading Conference.

Mason, J., and D. Dunning. 1986. Towards a model relating home literacy with beginning reading. Paper presented at the Annual Meeting of the

References

American Educational Research Assocation, San Francisco, CA, April 1986.

Mason, B. 2006. Free voluntary reading and autonomy in second language acquisition: Improving TOEFL scores from reading alone. *International Journal of Foreign Language Teaching* 2(1): 2–5.

Mason, B. 2011. Impressive gains on the TOEIC after one year of comprehensible input, with no output or grammar study. *The International Journal of Foreign Language Teaching* 7(1): 247–256.

Mason, B. 2013a. Substantial gains in listening and reading ability in English as a foreign language from voluntary listening and reading in a 75 year old student. *The International Journal of Foreign Language Teaching* 8(1): 25–27.

Mason, B. 2013b. The case of Mr. Kashihara: Another case of substantial gains in reading and listening without output or grammar study. *Shitennoji University Bulletin* 56: 417–428.

McCormick, C., and J. Mason. 1986. Intervention procedures for increasing preschool children's interest in and knowledge about reading. In W. Teale and E. Sulzby (eds.), *Emergent Literacy* (pp. 90–115). Norwood, NJ: Ablex.

McQuillan, J. 1988. *The Literacy Crisis: False Claims and Real Solutions.* Portsmouth, NH: Heinemann.

Mendelsohn A., L. Mogiler, B. Dreyer, J. Forman, S. Weinstein, M. Broderick, K. Cheng, T. Magloire, T. Moore, and C. Napier. 2001. The impact of a clinic-based literacy intervention on language development in inner-city preschool children. *Pediatrics* 107(1): 130–134.

Miller, D. 2009. *The Book Whisperer.* Hoboken, NJ: Jossey-Bass.

Mullis, I., M. Martin, A. Kennedy, and P. Foy. 2007. PIRLS 2006 international Report. Boston: International Study Center, Boston College.

Mullis, I., M. Martin, P. Foy, and K. Drucker. 2011. PIRLS 2011 International Results in Reading. Boston: International Study Center, Boston College.

Nagy, W., P. Herman, and R. Anderson. 1985. Learning words from context. *Reading Research Quarterly* 23: 6–50.

Nagy, W., R. Anderson, and P. Herman. 1987. Learning word meanings from context during normal reading. *American Educational Research Journal* 24: 237–270.

Nagy, W., and P. Herman. 1987. Breadth and depth of vocabulary knowledge: Implications for acquisition and instruction. In M. McKeown and M. Curtiss (eds.), *The Nature of Vocabulary Acquisition* (pp. 19–35). Hillsdale, NJ: Erbaum.

Nakanishi, T. 2014. A meta-analysis of extensive reading research. *TESOL Quarterly* 49(1), 6–37.

Nell, V. 1988. *Lost in a Book.* New Haven, CT: Yale University Press.

Neuman, S. 1986. The home environment and fifth-grade students' leisure reading. *Elementary School Journal* 86: 335–343.

Ohanian, S. 1999. *One Size Fits Few.* Portsmouth, NH: Heinemann.

Piastra, S., L. Justice, A. McGinty, and J. Kaderavek. 2012. Increasing young children's contact with print during shared reading: Longitudinal effects on literacy achievement. *Child Development* 83(3): 810–820.

Ravitch, D., and C. Finn. 1987. *What Do Our 17-Year-Olds Know?* New York: Harper and Row.

Ray, B., and C. Seely. 2008. *Fluency through TPR Storytelling*, 5th ed. Berkeley: Command Performance Language Institute.

Rosenblatt, R. 2001. *Rules for Aging.* Fort Washington, PA: Harvest Books.

Schleppegrell, M., M. Achugar, and T. Oteiz. 2004. The grammar of history: Enhancing content-based instruction through a functional focus on language. *TESOL Quarterly* 38(1): 67–93.

Scholastic. 2015. *Kids & Family Reading Report*, 5th ed. New York: Scholastic.

Schoonover, R. 1938. The case for voluminous reading. *English Journal* 27: 114–118.

Segal, J. 1997. Summer daze. Class paper, Trenton State University, Summer 1997.

Senechal, M., and J. LeFevre. 2002. Parent involvement in the development of children's reading skill: A five-year longitudinal study. *Child Development* 73(2): 445–460.

Shin, F., and S. Krashen. 2007. *Summer Reading: Program and Evidence.* New York: Allyn and Bacon.

Shu, H., R. C. Anderson, and H. Zhang. 1995. Incidental learning of word meanings while reading: A Chinese and American cross-cultural study. *Reading Research Quarterly* 30: 76–95.

Simonton, D. 1988. *Scientific Genius: A Psychology of Science.* Cambridge, MA: Harvard University Press.

Smith, F. 2004. *Understanding Reading,* 6th ed. Hillsdale, NJ: Erlbaum.

Southgate, V., H. Arnold, and S. Johnson. 1981. *Extending Beginning Reading.* London: Heinemann Educational Books.

Stanovich, K., and A. Cunningham. 1992. Studying the consequences of literacy within a literate society: The cognitive correlates of print exposure. *Memory and Cognition* 20(1): 51–68.

Stanovich, K., and A. Cunningham. 1993. Where does knowledge come from? Specific associations between print exposure and information acquisition. *Journal of Educational Psychology* 85(2): 211–229.

Stokes, J., S. Krashen, and J. Kartchner. 1998. Factors in the acquisition of the present subjunctive in Spanish: The role of reading and study. *ITL: Review of Applied Linguistics* 121–122: 19–25.

Sullivan, A., and M. Brown. 2013. *Social Inequalities in Cognitive Scores at age 16: The Role of Reading.* London: Centre for Longitudinal Studies, Institute of Education, University of London.

Sullivan, A., and M. Brown. 2014. *Vocabulary from Adolescence to Middle-Age.* London: Centre for Longitudinal Studies, Institute of Education, University of London.

Swales, J. 1990. *Genre Analysis: English in Academic and Research Settings.* Cambridge: Cambridge University Press.

Toppo, G., D. Vergano, and USA Today. 2009. Scientist shortage? Maybe not. ABC News. http://abcnews.go.com/Technology/story?id=8037674&page=1.

Trelease, J. 1995. *The Read-Aloud Handbook,* 3rd ed. New York: Penguin.

Trelease, J. 2001. *The Read-Aloud Handbook,* 4th ed. New York: Penguin.

References

Tse, S. K., R. Y. H. Lam, O. K. M. Ip, J. W. I. Lam, E. K. Y. Loh, and A. S. F. Tso. 2010. Family resources and students' reading attainment: Capitalising on home factors. *L1 Educational Studies in Language and Literature* 10(3): 27–54.

Tse, S. K., X. Y. Xiao, H. W. Ko, J. W. I. Lam, S. Y. Hui, and H. W. Ng. (2015). Do reading practices make a difference? The analysis of PIRLS data for Hong Kong and Taiwan fourth-grade students. *Compare: A Journal of Comparative and International Education.*

Tudball, L. 2010. Curriculum's narrow focus leaves students bereft of big ideas. *Sydney Morning Herald*, March 2, 2010. http://www.smh.com.au /federal-politics/political-opinion/curriculums-narrow-focus-leaves -students-bereft-of-big-ideas-20100301-pdi2.html.

Ujiie, J., and S. Krashen. 1996. Comic book reading, reading enjoyment, and pleasure reading among middle class and chapter I middle school students. *Reading Improvement* 33(1): 51–54.

Ujiie, J., and S. Krashen. 2002. Home run books and reading enjoyment. *Knowledge Quest* 31(1): 36–37.

Ujiie, J., and S. Krashen. 2005. Is "acclaimed" children's literature popular among children? A secondary analysis of Nilson, Peterson, and Searfoss (1980). *Knowledge Quest* 34(1): 39–40.

Ujiie, J., and S. Krashen. 2006. Are prizewinning books popular among children? An analysis of public library circulation. *Knowledge Quest* 34(3): 33–35.

Von Specken, D., J. Kim, and S. Krashen. 2000. The home run book: Can one positive reading experience create a reader? *California School Library Journal* 23(2): 8–9.

Vonnegut, K. 1997. *Timequake.* New York: Putnam Publishing Group.

Wang, F. Y., and S. Y. Lee. 2007. Storytelling is the bridge. *International Journal of Foreign Language Teaching* 3(2): 30–35.

Wertham, F. 1954. *Seduction of the Innocent.* New York: Rinehart.

Worthy, J., M. Moorman, and M. Tumer. 1999. What Johnny likes to read is hard to find in school. *Reading Research Quarterly* 34(1): 12–27.

Wright, R. 1966. *Black Boy.* New York: Harper and Row.

Zhao, Y. 2009. *Catching Up or Leading the Way? American Education in the Age of Globalization.* ASCD: Alexandria, VA.

Index

Author Biographies

Stephen D. Krashen

A highly influential and prolific author, linguist, and researcher, Stephen D. Krashen has written more than 500 books and articles in the fields of literacy, language acquisition, neurolinguistics, and bilingual education.

Krashen is a global advocate of reading and the importance of the role of reading in language acquisition, and his publications have received numerous awards, including the Mildenberger Award (Modern Language Association) and the Pimsleur Award (American Council of Foreign Language Teaching). In 2005, Krashen was added to the International Reading Association's Reading Hall of Fame. He is also the 1977 Incline Bench Press Champion of Venice Beach and currently trains at Gold's Gym.

Sy-Ying Lee

Sy-Ying Lee (syying.lee@mail.ntust.edu.tw) is currently a professor at National Taiwan University of Science and Technology, and chair of the Department of Applied Foreign Languages. Her research interests include issues related to second-language acquisition and literacy development, extensive reading, reader-text interaction, and blogging. She has published 30 professional papers in national and international scholarly journals and one monograph, and has made over 50 presentations in professional conferences throughout the world and has held more than 25 workshops for preservice and in-service teachers.

Dr. Lee has received the Outstanding Specialty Award given by the Taiwan Ministry of Science & Technology, and also the Teaching Excellence Award from National Taipei University.

She holds a PhD in Language and Literacy from the University of Southern California School of Education.

Christy Lao

Christy Lao is an associate professor of education, founding director of the Confucius Institute (CI) at San Francisco State University (SFSU), coordinator of the Chinese Bilingual Teacher Education Program, and the principal investigator and director of four major federal projects.

Lao has provided leadership in curriculum development and professional development in the areas of second-language acquisition, bilingual education, ESL methodology, Chinese language teaching pedagogy, reading, and biliteracy development.

She has published widely, with a focus on Chinese language learners. Previously, she was a faculty member at Teachers College, Columbia University, and at Hong Kong Baptist University. For the past 25 years, she has worked with Chinese bilingual schools and teachers in San Francisco, New York City, Hong Kong, and China.